THE *COMPLETE* BEGINNER'S GUIDE TO
SKIN DIVING

THE *COMPLETE* BEGINNER'S GUIDE TO

SKIN DIVING

by Shaney Frey

Foreword by Vice-Admiral C. B. Momsen

DOUBLEDAY & COMPANY, INC., GARDEN CITY, NEW YORK

Picture Credits

Photographs by Hank Frey: Pictures 1, 2, 3, 7, 9, 10, 11, 12, 13, 14, 18, 20, 21, 22, 23, 24, 25, 26, 30, 31, 32, 33, 36, 37, 41, 42, 44, 46, 47, 49, 51, 54, 59, 60, 61, 64, 66, 67, 68, 69, 70, 71, 72, 73, 74, 75, 76, 77, 78, 79, 80, 81, 82, 83, 84, 85, 87, and 99

Photographs by Paul J. Tzimoulis: Frontis and pictures 4, 5, 6, 8, 27, 28, 29, 34, 35, 38, 39, 43, 45, 48, 50, 52, 55, 62, 63, 65, and 98

Photographs courtesy of the Miami Seaquarium: Pictures 40 and 53

Photographs by Burton McNeely: Pictures 56 and 88

Photograph by Marine Studios, Marineland, Florida: Picture 89

Official Photographs, United States Navy: Pictures 90, 91, and 97

Photograph by Jacques Ertaud, © by National Geographic Society: Picture 92

Photographs by Bates Littlehales, © by National Geographic Society: Pictures 93, 95, and 96

Photograph by Robert Goodman, © by National Geographic Society: Picture 94

Photograph by Treat Davidson, courtesy National Audubon Society: Picture 57

Photograph by Dade Thornton, courtesy National Audubon Society: Picture 58

Drawings by Shaney Frey: Pictures 15, 16, 17, 19, 86 and diagrams for 69, 70, 72, and 74

Library of Congress Catalog Card Number 65-11061
Copyright © 1965 by Shaney Frey
All Rights Reserved
Printed in the United States of America

ACKNOWLEDGMENTS

I wish to thank the youngsters—and their parents—who gave generously of their time and effort: Douglas Cioce, Jay Freiday, Jr., Gerry Gironda, Richard Glauber, Patricia and Scott Smithline, Erwin and Neil Stockel, Andrew Stockwell, Brant Whelan.

My grateful thanks for special assistance, suggestions, and criticism to: Dr. Fitzhugh W. Boggs, Research Associate, United States Rubber Company; John R. Clark, President, American Littoral Society; Joe Dorsey, Diver's Den, Baltimore, Maryland; Dr. H. Harry Hoehn, Scuba instructor, Queens College; Dr. Carleton Ray, New York Zoological Society; Captain Walter F. Mazzone, United States Naval Medical Research Laboratory, New London, Connecticut; and Commander R. D. Workman, United States Naval Experimental Diving Unit, Washington, D.C.

For their co-operation in supplying equipment on short notice and at odd hours, I also wish to thank: the management of the Allenhurst Beach Club, New Jersey; John and Joe Shuck at Cougar Sports, Bronx, New York; Michael and Victor Hritz at the Crystal Aquarium, Manhattan, New York; and Jack and Kevin Cunningham at Readers, Manhattan, New York.

Special thanks for allowing us to invade the peace and privacy of their homes and pools to: Jay Gordon Freiday; Tom Parise, Jr.; and Mr. and Mrs. Guy Parsons.

To Charlie Smithline, Manager, Underwater Division, Seamless Rubber Company, goes my deep appreciation for his hard work and unfailing assistance in obtaining equipment and models, for arranging photography sessions, and for his expert technical advice and constant encouragement.

To Paul Tzimoulis, Eastern manager, *Skin Diver Magazine,* goes my sincere appreciation for providing photographs.

To Burton McNeely, grateful thanks for providing essential photographs on a moment's notice.

To Hank Frey, especial thanks for photographs and for enduring calmly a disrupted household.

I am indebted to Duke Pontin for working so hard to provide an exciting cover for this book. And to Captain Herb and Chris Pontin, Sea Center, Big Pine Key, Florida and Captain Craig Pontin, Sea Center, Upper Key Largo, Florida, for their cheerful assistance.

to my two young skin divers
KATHLEEN and CHRISTOPHER

CONTENTS

FOREWORD

For many centuries, the water world remained a dim, silent place of mystery. Although people traveled across the surface in swift boats and swam leisurely atop the water, they had little or no idea that an amazing, mercurial world exists below the surface. The surface was like a window shade pulled down to shut out the view. Modern skin diving equipment has opened the window wide to reveal the splendid view. Millions of former surface-skimmers have become underwater explorers and have discovered a watery world filled with wonders: beautiful plants; colorful sponges and corals; weird and handsome animals of all sizes and shapes. It is not surprising that the sport of skin diving is the fastest-growing sport in the world— for the young and the old.

The relatively new equipment which allows you to explore the underwater world also aids scientific research below the surface. Bear in mind that the oceans cover over 70 per cent of the earth's surface. Vast unused resources are contained over, in, on the bottom of, and in the earth's crust below these oceans. The sun and winds evaporate and distribute fresh water in great quantities but less than 1 per cent is actually used by the people on earth. The latent power in the winds, tides, waves and currents of the seas is completely un-used by man. The resources of the sea could provide all that would be needed to care for the world's expanding population. Also, salt water is an almost ideal shield against radiation. There are over 40 different minerals and chemicals in solution in the 330 million cubic miles of sea water. For instance, it has been estimated that every cubic mile of sea water contains over 70 million dollars worth of gold!

It is no wonder that wise men are becoming acutely interested in oceanography. This book by Shaney Frey is aimed at a future generation—your generation. The author, who is an expert skin and scuba diver, presents the material in a fascinating way. It will serve a very useful purpose if it stimulates your interest in the study of the oceans. If you, who at this moment are about to embark on a new and thrilling sport, were to carry this new skill, skin diving, to your adult years and your professional life, then this book is truly worth while.

Vice-Admiral Charles B. Momsen, USN Ret.

St. Petersburg, Florida
1964

THE *COMPLETE* BEGINNER'S GUIDE TO
SKIN DIVING

Picture 1 Diving mask

CHAPTER ONE

Equipment and How to Choose It

There are many interesting and exciting things you can do as a skin diver. You can watch fish at work and play. You can collect small, colorful fish for a salt-water aquarium. You can learn to photograph the unusual animals and strange scenery found in the underwater world. You can help to collect and record information about marine life for scientific study.

All this—and more—is made possible by simple skin diving equipment:

The Mask is like a small personal window. (*Picture 1*) The glass face plate keeps the water away from your eyes and nose, and allows you to see clearly the wonderful world beneath the surface. The mask should have clear, shatterproof glass bound by a stainless steel rim. Masks which have tinted face plates make it harder to see clearly underwater, so they are not really useful. Masks which have plastic face plates scratch easily and also cannot be defogged properly, so they are not very useful either.

The rubber portion of the mask should be of good quality rubber that is slightly flexible. Masks which are made of very soft rubber will collapse underwater. They will constantly fill with water. Hard rubber or plastic masks are uncomfortable.

Obviously, masks which combine soft rubber and tinted plastic face plates are useless to a serious skin diver.

To make sure your new mask fits properly, try it on without using the headstrap. Inhale a little through your nose. If the mask stays in place without being held, then it will be leakproof.

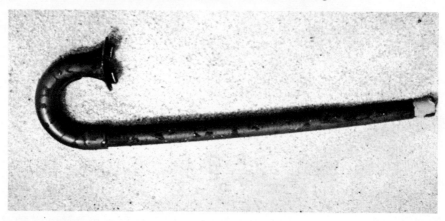

Picture 2 Snorkel

The Snorkel lets you breathe easily while you swim on or just below the surface admiring the sights below through your mask. (*Picture 2*)

The snorkel should be a simple J-shape. It should be about sixteen inches long. Snorkels longer than sixteen inches make it very difficult to breathe, so these are not practical. Snorkels which have little "bird cages" on top are pretty fancy—but they don't do the job very well. The ball trapped in the little cage sometimes gets stuck so that it is impossible to get any air at all. A two-in-one combination of mask and snorkel looks like something out of this world, but it is not much use in the water world. It is harder to breathe through a mask-snorkel combination. Also, if the mask leaks, you will not get air at all, only water.

The snorkel mouthpiece must be comfortable. You may be able to judge the correct size mouthpiece just by looking at it, or better still, you can measure the width of the mouthpiece by placing your thumb and forefinger on either end of it and, holding your fingers that far apart, measure them against your mouth. If your finger tips touch the corners of your mouth the snorkel mouthpiece is too small. Water will leak into your mouth and eventually you will lose your grip on the mouthpiece. If your finger tips touch your face just about three-eighths of an inch, or a little less, on either side of your mouth, it will be close to a perfect fit. A larger mouthpiece will be difficult to get into your mouth and may cause very tired, sore mouth and jaw muscles.

Picture 3 Fins

The Fins increase your leg-power threefold, causing you to move faster and farther with slow, relaxed movement. (*Picture 3*) They should fit as well as a good pair of shoes. Beginning divers should have fairly soft fins. Then after the leg muscles have grown strong and accustomed to swimming underwater, harder fins can be used.

Some fins have closed heels and toes. Some have closed heels and open toes. Some have open heels and open toes. Any one of these is fine, just as long as the fins fit properly. Fins which are too tight can cause foot cramps. Fins which are too loose can either fall off or rub blisters on the feet and can cause leg cramps. Before buying, try the fins on just as you would a pair of shoes.

Mask, fins, and snorkel are all you need to learn skin diving in a swimming pool. But before you graduate from the pool to open water you must learn how to use safety equipment and other accessories.

The Safety Vest is by far the most important piece of skin diving equipment. It should be made of rubberized fabric. It should have a CO_2 (carbon dioxide) cartridge and a mouth inflation valve. (*Picture 4*)

The CO_2 cartridge can be "popped" to inflate the vest quickly in an emergency. The inflated vest will float you safely on the surface with your head above water, and will make it much easier for you to swim back to shore.

The mouth inflation valve can be used if you grow tired. You can also blow air into the vest by mouth if it should ever leak after popping the cartridge, or if the cartridge itself should be a dud.

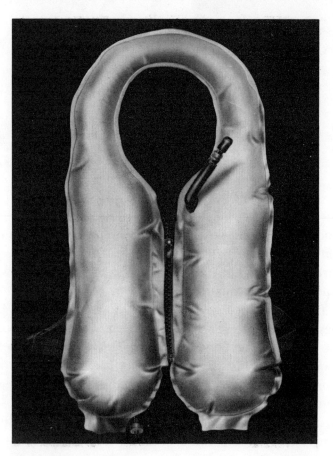

Picture 4 Safety vest

The Diver's Flag and Surface Float are essential to safe skin diving. (*Picture 5*) The flag will protect you from boat traffic. The float will be your own portable island, a resting place whenever you or your buddy become tired.

Picture 5 Diver's flag and float

Diver's flags are sold at all dive shops. Many shops also sell surface floats. The bright red-orange flag with a diagonal white stripe means DIVER BELOW. It warns boats to stay at least one hundred feet away. You must remain within one hundred feet of the flag for protection. The flag should be attached to a mast at least three feet high. Attach the mast securely to your surface float.

The surface float can be a *good* inner tube, a one- or two-man life raft, an air mattress, or a surfboard. Inner tubes are the least expensive. But they are reliable only as long as they have no patches.

Tie a fifty-foot length of nylon line to your surface float. You can tow the flag and float as you skin dive and stay well within the protective one-hundred-foot mark.

The Skin Diver's Knife is used to cut yourself free from any entanglement. If you are careful—and watch where you are swimming —the chances of becoming entangled are very small. But always have your knife handy just in case. The knife is *definitely not a weapon* to be used against marine life!

The knife should have a stainless steel blade, with saw teeth on one edge and one smooth edge. Test your knife. The saw edge must cut quickly and easily through rope or fishing line.

Wear the knife on either your calf or thigh where it can be reached easily. Most diver's knives have leg straps on the sheath. (*Picture 6*)

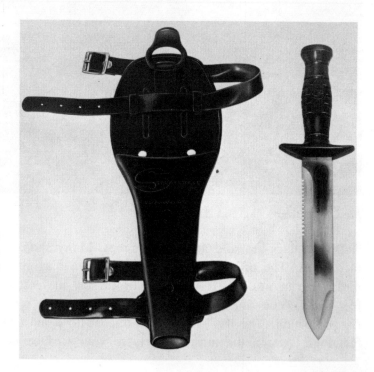

Picture 6
Skin diver's
knife

Picture 7 Wet suit

The Wet Suit *must* be worn in cold water. Without it you will become too cold. The cold will make you shiver. The shivering uses up a lot of calories, and you become very tired. A *tired* skin diver is not a *safe* skin diver.

You need protective clothing in water colder than 80° Fahrenheit. The *Neoprene wet suit* provides the best protection against coldness. The wet suit consists of shirt, pants, hood, boots, and mitts. (*Picture 7*) When the water temperature is between 70° and 80° you need only the wet shirt. Below 70° you must wear the entire suit.

Most wet suits are three-sixteenths of an inch thick. Tiny air spaces trapped in the Neoprene provide insulation against cold water. A little bit of water seeps into the suit. It becomes trapped and heated by your body. But a *lot* of water will chill you. Your wet suit should fit you snugly so that water cannot get into it easily. Snug does not mean tight. If your suit is too tight you will not have enough freedom of movement to swim well.

Be careful not to tear the wet suit with your fingernails when putting it on. Use the flat palms of your hands to work on the sleeves and the pant legs. The suit will go on more easily if you sprinkle specially manufactured powder inside the suit and on your arms and legs. The special powder is available at all skin diving equipment shops. Neoprene suits which are lined with nylon do not require powdering. If you *do* tear the suit it is, fortunately, easy to repair. You can buy a small can of Neoprene cement at a dive shop. Brush some cement on each side of the tear. When the cement looks dull, press the two sides of the tear together. Wait at least two hours before you use the suit again.

The Weight Belt (*Picture 8*) is necessary to offset the buoyancy of the wet suit. Weight is not needed if you are not wearing protective clothing.

The amount of weight you need depends on your size and on the amount of protective clothing you wear. You will need more weight when you dive in *salt* water than you will in *fresh* water. Salt water is more buoyant.

Always test the amount of weight you are wearing in waist-high water before you begin to skin dive. The proper amount of weight will allow you to float easily on the surface. You will be able to surface dive with little effort. Try using about nine pounds in salt water with a full wet suit, and about six pounds in fresh water. The proper

Picture 8 Weight belt

amount for you may be a little more or a little less. But these amounts will be fairly close. You need only about half the weight if you wear just the wet shirt.

Your weight belt must have a quick-release hitch or buckle. You must be able to remove the weight belt instantly in an emergency. And you must be able to unfasten the belt easily with one or two fingers.

How to Care for Your Equipment: After each day of skin diving, wash all of your equipment with clean, fresh water, particularly after diving in salt water. Wet all equipment and dry thoroughly. Sprinkle the special powder inside your wet suit. Don't use any other powder which contains oil or perfume because it will ruin your wet suit. Store the suit on a hanger in a dry, cool place along with the rest of your skin diving equipment.

The First-aid Kit will complete your equipment list. Skin diving is not a dangerous sport as long as you are well-trained and careful. The first-aid kit is recommended because, as with many other outdoor sports, you may cut a finger or scratch yourself, and it may be a long way to a first-aid station or a doctor's office. Of course, always call a doctor for a serious accident.

The first-aid kit should be kept in the boat, on the shore, or on your float. It should contain 4″ by 4″ compresses, tweezers, gauze bandages, adhesive tape, small scissors, small adhesive bandages, smelling salts, iodine or Merthiolate, burn ointment, an eye cup and eye wash, and ammonia.

Tape four dimes to the inside of the kit along with the phone numbers of the nearest doctor, hospital, first-aid station, and police department. You may never need any of these—but in case of an accident they are well worth having on hand.

Learn to give artificial respiration and be sure your diving buddy does the same. The mouth-to-mouth technique is considered the most practical method. Lifesaving and Water Safety courses for juniors are given by some local American Red Cross chapters. You will find them listed in the phone book.

Before you begin skin diving instruction, go to your doctor for a complete medical checkup. You should not skin dive if you have any ear, nose, or throat ailment. Your heart and lungs must be sound and healthy.

When your doctor gives you a clean bill of health, you can go ahead with skin diving instruction—*providing you are a good swimmer.* You must be a good swimmer before you can become a skin diver. The instructor will ask you to:
– float or bob on the surface for twenty minutes
– swim three hundred yards on the surface
– swim forty feet underwater
You must be able to do all this without using the skin diving equipment.

Ask at your local skin diving equipment store about a qualified instructor. Or at the YMCA or YMHA. Try to find a friend who will learn with you. He—or she—can then be your diving buddy.

You will improve your personal safety and watermanship if you take an American Red Cross Junior Lifesaving course. Learn to dive from a qualified instructor if possible—or from a competent adult diver. Practice all skin diving skills thoroughly in a pool or in clear, shallow water free of boat traffic before you go into open water.

CHAPTER TWO

Learning to Skin Dive

You know about the equipment you need. Now—how do you learn to skin dive?

The most important rule for skin divers of any age is NEVER DIVE ALONE. Always have an adult nearby. Learn and practice skin diving in a clear, clean swimming pool. The best way to learn is to take lessons under the watchful eye of an experienced skin diving instructor, and these are the skills you will be taught:

First, and this sounds funny, spit in your mask. Why? Because otherwise the glass will get foggy and you will not be able to see clearly underwater. Why does a mask get foggy? The air in the mask is heated by your body. The moisture of your breath causes humidity, or water vapor, inside the mask. This warm water vapor forms water droplets when the outside of the mask is colder than the inside. The droplets collect on the glass plate and you can't see through them. This is where the saliva is helpful: chemicals in your saliva prevent the water from forming into many tiny droplets. Instead, the water forms a thin, smooth film through which you can see.

Dip your mask in the water. Then spit lots of saliva inside the mask and rub it all over the glass plate. Now rinse the mask again. Put the mask on, being careful not to twist the headstrap.

Next, slip the snorkel under the headstrap and grip the prongs of the mouthpiece firmly between your teeth. (*Picture 9*) Your lips act as a seal to keep the water out of the mouthpiece.

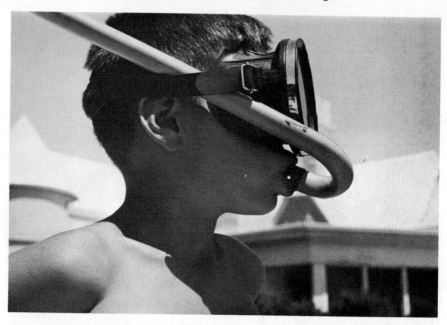

Picture 9 Correct position of snorkel

Practice breathing through the snorkel while standing in waist-deep water. (*Picture 10*) Put your face in the water and breathe evenly through your mouth. It takes a little while to become accustomed to breathing through your mouth rather than your nose.

Now take a deep breath through the snorkel, hold it, and let yourself sink toward the bottom of the pool. Your head and the entire snorkel go all the way under the water. Now lift your head just until the top of the snorkel is a few inches above water, and blow hard into the mouthpiece—just as if you were blowing out a dozen candles on a birthday cake. The water shoots out of the snorkel like a water fountain spout. (*Picture 11*) Now the snorkel is free of water. Take a breath of air without lifting your head out of the water. Practice until it is very easy to clear your snorkel.

Why do skin divers use a snorkel? Mainly because it is easier and less tiring to swim with your head *in* the water. Without the snorkel you have to keep lifting your head above the surface to breathe. Also, when using the snorkel you are able to keep a constant watch on the scenery below you. When you want a closer look at some interesting plant or animal, you can keep it in sight as you

Picture 10 Breathing through the snorkel

surface dive. You take a deep breath through your snorkel at the surface, hold it, and surface dive. Once underwater, you are simply holding your breath—just as you would without a snorkel. You barely notice the snorkel mouthpiece. The snorkel does not hinder your

Picture 11 Blowing air out through snorkel

movement underwater. You look up as you return to the surface to be sure nothing is in your way. At the surface you exhale through the snorkel. You begin breathing normally without raising your head above water and continue exploring the scenery below.

Sometimes water seeps into the mask. When this happens, raise your head above water and lift the bottom of the mask away from your face. The water runs out. Then refit the mask on your face to get a better watertight seal.

Next you will learn to use your fins. Wet both feet and the fins before putting the fins on. This makes the fins slip on easily. Push the fin on your foot with both hands as far as it will go. (*Picture 12*) Then, using both thumbs like a shoehorn, slip the heel of the fin over the heel of your foot.

You are now ready to practice the leg kicks while holding on to the side of the pool. First you will learn the *flutter kick*. Practice moving your legs from the hips. (*Picture 13*) Bend your knees very slightly. Your legs should move up and down about twenty times a minute. Be careful to keep your fins under the water—they will not do their work as well if they break the surface.

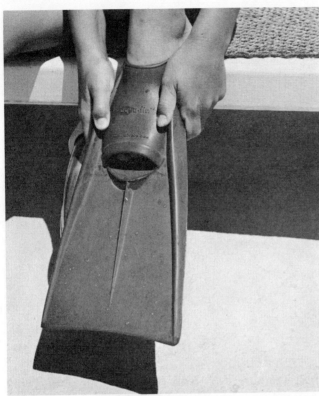

Picture 12
Putting on fins

Picture 13
The flutter kick

Picture 14 The side kick

Next, the *side kick*. (*Picture 14*) Roll over on your side, being sure the top of the snorkel remains above water. Move your legs just about the same as if you were pedaling a bicycle. When you are out skin diving, you will want to alternate between the flutter kick and the side kick in order to rest your leg muscles.

Now you are ready for a practice session using your two new skills, snorkel breathing and leg kicks. Let go of the side of the pool, and swim back and forth, keeping your arms at your sides and using only the fins to move through the water. It is not necessary to use your arms in a swimming stroke—in fact, using your arms would be a needless waste of energy. You must learn to imitate the fish you will see in open water. Their smooth, sleek forms are designed to move easily through the water. You will be more fishlike with your arms close to your sides or held straight out in front of your body. The fins will provide more than enough speed and agility, leaving your hands free to carry a camera or other equipment. Concentrate on keeping the fins below the surface and moving smoothly through the water.

You are *almost* ready to learn the next skill, but first you must know a little bit about water pressure.

Although you don't feel it, there is pressure pushing against your body all the time. At sea level there are *14.7 pounds of pressure pushing against each square inch* of your head, arms, legs—everywhere. This is called *atmospheric* pressure. It is simply caused by the weight of the air above and around you. You breathe this air. So the pressure *inside* your body equals the pressure *outside* your body.

You must remember that on land you live under *one atmosphere* of pressure, which is equal to 14.7 pounds per square inch, or 14.7 psi.

Water weighs more than air. Fresh water 33 feet deep also causes a pressure of 14.7 pounds per square inch. Do a little arithmetic.

Add: the *atmospheric* pressure   14.7 psi
                 to
the *water* pressure   14.7 psi
the sum is *absolute* pressure.   29.4 psi

(If *one atmosphere* equals 14.7 psi then *two atmospheres* equal 29.4 psi.)

Since the absolute pressure in thirty-three feet of water is equal to *two atmospheres,* eleven feet is thus equal to one third of this, or 9.8 psi. Sixteen feet is equal to about one atmosphere, or 14.7 psi.

Pressure in salt water is just a little different—a pound or so higher.

You should not dive deeper than eleven feet until you have had at least a year's experience, and even then, you should seldom go below sixteen feet.

Before you can dive safely, you must learn how to make the air pressure inside your ears equal to the pressure in the water outside your ears. Otherwise, you will injure your eardrums. This is called *clearing the ears,* or *equalizing the pressure* in the ears. At eleven feet, for example, you must increase the pressure inside your ears 9.8 psi to equalize the pressure. This can be done by any one of three methods. Practice and use whichever one feels best to you:

(1) Put on the mask, fins, and snorkel and go into the pool. Take a deep breath through the snorkel and pull yourself slowly down

the pool ladder. A few feet below the surface you will begin to feel pressure on your ears. Right away *hold the mask against your face and blow air through your nose into the mask.* You will hear a "pop" or "squeak" in your ears. The feeling of pressure against your ears will disappear. When you go down a few more feet you will feel pressure again. Equalize again.

(2) Try another method. When you begin to feel pressure, *push the bottom of your mask up against your nose to close your nostrils. Then blow through your nose* against the closed nostrils. Again, your ears will "pop" or "squeak."

(3) To equalize the pressure in your ears when wearing a nose-pinch mask, all you have to do is *pinch your nose closed with thumb and forefinger, and blow through your nose.*

Each of these methods helps to open the small air tubes (the Eustachian tubes) in your throat so that air can travel more easily from the lungs to the ear spaces. Since the air in the lungs is compressed by the water pressure, the air pressure inside the ears will be equal to the water pressure.

There is one important thing to remember. If you ever find it difficult to equalize the pressure in your ears, go *up* a few feet and try again. Don't go any deeper until you have equalized. *Don't try to force it!*

A head cold will make it practically impossible for you to clear your ears. Give up diving for a while. Wait until you have gotten over the cold before you go skin diving.

As you surface dive, your mask may begin to feel tight. Blow a little air through your nose into the mask to equalize the air pressure inside the mask.

Never wear earplugs or goggles when you skin dive! Air would be trapped between the earplug and your eardrum. This air would remain at atmospheric pressure. But the air inside your ear and the water outside the earplug would be at a higher pressure. One of two serious accidents would happen: either the earplug would be jammed far down into your ear canal, or your eardrum would rupture. Earplugs are *out!*

Goggles are also *out!* You cannot equalize the pressure inside goggles because they do not cover your nose. Water pressure can push the goggles hard against your eyes, causing serious injury.

Now that you know how to breathe through your snorkel, swim with your fins, and equalize the pressure in your ears, it is time to learn how to surface dive.

There are three standard surface dives you should learn. The first is called the *tuck:* snorkel along the surface . . . take a deep breath . . . quickly tuck your knees up to your chest . . . roll your body forward and down . . . and straighten your legs so that they are sticking up out of the water. The weight of your legs *above* water pushes you deeper *into* the water. Remember to equalize your ears as you kick your way down to the bottom. (*Picture 15*)

The second surface dive is the *pike:* as before, snorkel along the surface . . . take a deep breath through your snorkel . . . bend at the waist . . . and lift your hips while keeping your legs straight . . . then point your legs up and arch your back. The weight of your hips and legs pushes you deeper, and you will glide gracefully under the water. (*Picture 16*)

The third dive is the *feet-first* dive: from a "standing" position, push yourself *up* by kicking hard with your fins . . . at the same

Picture 15 Diagram of the tuck dive

Picture 16 Diagram of the pike dive

time, push down against the water with your hands . . . this brings you chest-high above the surface . . . then let yourself sink down into the water with your hands at your sides . . . when your head is below water, move yourself deeper by pushing up against the water with your hands . . . bend at the waist and equalize your ears as you glide farther down. Swim slowly along the bottom of the pool using the flutter kick. (*Picture 17*)

Look up as you return to the surface. When you are skin diving in open water, you will want to be sure you are not going to "surface" under a boat, or run into another diver. Just as you look before crossing the street, you *must* look up to see that your path to the surface is clear.

Now put all your new skills together. Wet your feet and fins. Put your fins on. Defog your mask (remember: rinse, spit in the mask, and rinse again). Put the mask on and slip the snorkel under the headstrap. Go into the shallow end of the pool and begin the flutter kick. Now take a deep breath, hold it, and do a *tuck*. As you return to the surface, look up and you will see that your image is reflected by the underside of the surface, just like a mirror. Although you cannot see it, when your head breaks the surface, the reflection is shat-

Picture 17 Diagram of the feet-first dive

tered just like broken glass. (Watch your instructor's reflection as he surfaces.) Clear your snorkel. The water will shoot high above your head. Swim, using the flutter kick, to the side of the pool to learn the last skin diving skill—how to enter the deep end of the swimming pool wearing mask, fins, and snorkel.

You must never dive headfirst into the water when wearing a mask.

Hold the mask and snorkel in place with one hand so that they will not be pushed off when you enter the water. Take a deep breath through the snorkel, and step off the edge of the pool—just as if you were going to walk into the corner candy store—and go straight down into the water. (*Picture 18*) Now, with a few gentle kicks, you float up to the surface and clear your snorkel. Use the newly learned flutter kick to glide easily across the length of the pool.

You now have your skin diving skills down pat. Your skin diving equipment is simple and practical, and includes a reliable safety vest. You have practiced inflating it both orally and using the CO_2 cartridge. Now all you have to do is to learn a few basic hand signals

Picture 18 Correct way to enter the water

so you can communicate with your buddy. Then you will be ready for your introduction to skin diving in open water.

It is important to have a diving buddy in open water—a buddy who is a *skilled* diver, just as you must be. You will look out for one another. If you get into trouble, your buddy must be able to help you—and vice versa! *Always stay within sight of your diving buddy.*

You cannot talk underwater, but you *can* use hand signals. This sign language is useful during an ordinary day of diving. It can be a valuable means of underwater communication in an emergency. You should memorize and practice these hand signals (*Picture 19*) and the ones you learn from your instructor with a skin diving buddy in the swimming pool:

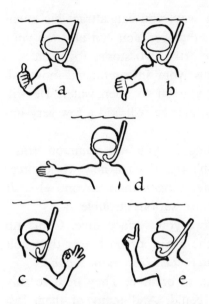
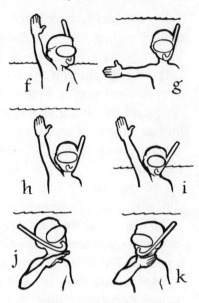

Picture 19 Underwater hand signals

(a) Thumbs up — Go up

(b) Thumbs down — Go down

(c) Thumb and first finger joined in a circle — Everything is okay, or okay, I understand

(d) Arm straight out to the side, palm up — I don't understand your signal

(e) First finger of right hand pointed up, moving arm up and down rapidly — Danger overhead

(f) Right arm straight overhead, rotated in circle (on the surface) — Assemble here

(g) Right arm out to side, rotated in circle with palm out — Dangerous marine life

(h) Right arm held straight up, palm out (underwater) — Help me

(i) Right arm held straight up, palm out (on surface) — Pick me up

(j) Slashing motion across throat — I am fouled

(k) One hand clutching throat — I am hurt

If your buddy is not looking your way, you can attract his attention by yelling into your snorkel mouthpiece. You can also tap your knife against a hard object, or even strike two stones together.

Having taught you the hand signals, your instructor will now call for one final session before sending you off to open water. He will review all the skin diving safety rules, and he will add a few very important words of caution:

Skin diving is a safe sport as long as you use common sense. Please *don't try to be a "hero."* Don't try to set a new world's record by attempting to stay underwater longer than anyone else. If you do, you are bound to get into serious trouble.

Take a normally deep breath before you surface dive. Come up as soon as you feel the need to breathe again, or no longer than half a minute. *Don't try to stay underwater "just one more second."*

Some divers have ignored the urge to breathe. They tried to stay underwater longer than they safely could. And many of them lost consciousness—and drowned. Certainly, trying to show off isn't worth your life or your buddy's.

If you try to swim farther underwater than another skin diver, the excitement is likely to make you overlook the natural urge to breathe. This kind of competition is senseless and dangerous.

Do you feel that you will have to compete with your diving buddies in some way? Okay—see who can do the smoothest surface dive, or who takes the best underwater photographs. But, please, *keep any competition sensible and safe.*

Armed with practiced skin diving skills and a sound knowledge of safety rules, you are ready to be introduced to open water, and a new world of fun and adventure.

Observe these important safety rules at all times:
  Always dive with a buddy—never dive alone
  Wear a safety vest on every dive
  Use a diver's flag and a reliable surface float
  Equalize your ears properly
  Never dive when you feel tired or sick
  Look up as you surface
  DON'T STAY UNDERWATER LONGER THAN HALF A MINUTE
  CAUTION: *Do not use goggles or earplugs when skin diving.*

CHAPTER THREE

Exploring History Underwater

All over the world, skin divers are discovering fragments of history. Scott is one of these underwater explorers. His dad, an expert diver, taught him all the skills you have just read about in Chapter Two. Scott also learned how to use essential safety equipment: the diver's flag, a surface float, and a safety vest. This equipment is required to skin dive safely in open water. Open water is any body of water other than a swimming pool. It can be a lake, quarry, river, spring, stream, or the huge ocean. In cold water, Scott wears a skin diver's wet suit and a weight belt.

Scott's dad decided that he was ready to do some real underwater exploring. He chose a large and interesting body of water in New York State—Lake George. Lake George is about thirty-six miles long and almost three miles across at its widest points. Scattered over the lake are more than two hundred small islands. To the average sightseer, Lake George offers boat trips and beautiful scenery. The skin diver finds much more beneath the surface, for Lake George was the scene of many battles. Here, Iroquois Indians fought rival northern tribes. British and colonial troops, aided by Indian allies, fought the French. Several forts were built. Through the years and the many battles, ships and weapons of war collected on the muddy bottom of Lake George.

When Scott and his dad decide to go exploring in cold water, they prepare for it carefully and thoroughly. First, Scott must put on a wet suit (made of foam Neoprene). Without the suit he would become too cold and tired to use his skin diving skills safely

Scott has learned to powder the inside of his suit so that it will be easier to slip on. He also sprinkles the special powder on his arms and legs. He works the pants on carefully with the palms of his hands to avoid ripping the Neoprene. (*Picture 20*) Next, he powders and puts on the shirt and then the boots. The hood and the mitts will wait until after he has put on the rest of his skin diving gear.

Picture 20 Putting on wet suit

Next Scott puts on the most important piece of skin diving equipment, the safety vest. (*Picture 21*) All the other equipment is designed to help him explore the *under*water world. The safety vest is designed to keep him safely on the *surface* should he ever run into trouble.

No one—not you or Scott or Scott's dad—should ever go into the water without this piece of lifesaving equipment.

Picture 21 Putting on safety vest

Scott must wear a weight belt over his wet suit. The wet suit makes him buoyant and he can float easily on the surface. But without extra weight he will tire himself out struggling to get below the surface. Scott puts the molded weights on his belt, and goes into waist-deep water to test his belt. He still floats easily on the surface. But he can also get beneath the surface without struggling. The amount of weight is just about right. Too much weight would have pulled him under, and that, of course, is dangerous. Scott's dad is very strict about testing the amount of weight before each dive because it is so important to Scott's safety.

All weight belts must have a quick-release buckle. You must be able to unfasten the belt *quickly* with one hand. (*Picture 22*)

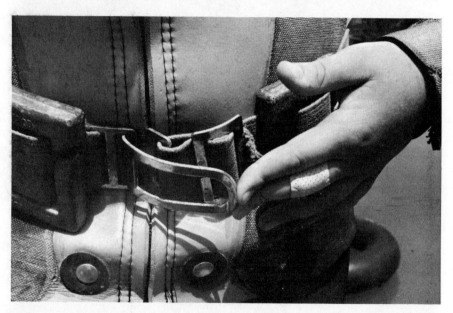

Picture 22 Weight belt in place

Scott and his dad have a surface float and a diver's flag. Their float is a good inner tube, their own portable island. They can rest on it, and it can carry extra equipment, such as a camera or a speargun. They hope it will be needed to carry back at least one interesting discovery.

The diver's flag is attached to the surface float. This flag is especially important when diving in waters where there is a lot of boat traffic. Scott's dad has tied a line to the float. He can tow both the float and the flag along with them.

Scott puts on his fins, which are slightly larger than normal to fit over his boots. Then he puts on the hood, defogs his mask, and puts it on. He slips the snorkel under the headstrap and finally puts his mitts on. He is ready to dive. He and his diving buddy, in this case his dad, enter the water. (*Picture 23*)

Picture 23 Ready to enter the water

Visibility is fair. Scott can see underwater for about fifteen feet. As he snorkels along the surface, he sees the sloping, grassy bottom, and a dim, dark shape. He surface dives for a better look. He finds what looks like a growth-covered, half-buried Indian canoe lying on

Picture 24 Finding buried canoe

Picture 25 Finding a cutlass

its side. (*Picture 24*) Scott and his diving buddy go up to the surface for air and dive again. They look for unnatural mounds and shapes around the canoe. They come upon a lot of scattered rocks and peculiar-shaped humps in the mud. As Scott returns to the surface, he has a brief glimpse of an odd, long, skinny shape nearby. On the surface Scott tells his dad that he saw a strange object just below. They surface dive together and dig down into the mud. Scott sees his dad grin around his snorkel mouthpiece as he pulls the object free of the clinging mud. Within a few seconds ten-year-old Scott holds in his hands a weapon which today is worn only by high-ranking naval officers, but many years ago was a sailor's weapon on war vessels. He has discovered a cutlass—a short, heavy curved sword! (*Picture 25*)

The story could end here—for Scott was lucky to find such a small treasure in such a big lake. But he was doubly lucky. Five minutes later, Scott found a rusted musket that is almost two hundred years old! (*Picture 26*)

Picture 26 Divers with cutlass and musket (note mitts!)

It was an exciting day for Scott, and he was very proud indeed when he donated his finds to a museum. And Scott is not the exception. You read in the newspapers about skin divers who make valuable discoveries. You hear about them over the radio and on television. And when you get together with other skin divers you will hear tales of adventure and exploration from them.

You have a lot to look forward to. Among the most fascinating sights to be found in the sea is a shipwreck. They are not always easy to find. Some very old wooden vessels are no more than a lumpy distortion of the otherwise fairly smooth floor of the salty ocean. But the "newer" metal ships are weird and lovely submerged museums. They are covered with plant growth and anemones in northern waters, and with a crust of coral in southern seas. But north or south, in fresh water or salt water, they are always inhabited by many kinds of underwater life.

You must always be careful when exploring a shipwreck. The torn, jagged metal can be as sharp as the blade of a knife. A coral crust can cause serious cuts. Patches of fire coral are often found on tropical wrecks. *Always wear gloves.* And wear a wet suit when the water is cold.

If you happen to find a "new" wreck, one that still looks like a ship, be very careful. (*Pictures 27, 28, 29*) Stay outside. If you try to explore the inside of such a wreck you may find yourself trapped inside by a rusty door or hatch cover. You should always have an *adult* diving buddy within sight of you.

And who knows, *you* may find an old and valuable musket. But please don't decide to tear the wreck apart. Leave it as an underwater museum for other divers to see and enjoy. More important, leave it as you found it, as a home for fish. There is now a movement underway by the American Littoral Society (see Chapter Nine) to protect and preserve sunken wrecks as "cities of fish." Wrecks are important to the protection of underwater animals. They offer shelter where none may have existed before. Surely a sunken ship is of more value as shelter for homeless fish than as hundreds of souvenirs on hundreds of dusty shelves. There is still a lot of room for you to explore and investigate, without destroying something so valuable.

Picture 27 Exploring around a wreck

Picture 28 Exploring around sunken anchor

Picture 29 Careful survey of submerged wreck

While you are exploring, keep in mind the safety rules you have learned in these chapters:

Always wear a full wet suit in cold water (70° F or colder)
Always wear a wet shirt in water from 70° to 80° F
Always use a safety quick-release hitch on your weight belt
Check your weights in waist-high water
Wear gloves when exploring a wreck
Never go inside a wreck
Always dive with an adult diving buddy

Picture 30 Underwater photographer

CHAPTER FOUR

Underwater Photography

You can become an underwater photographer. (*Picture 30*) All you need is fairly clear water, either a simple underwater camera or a regular camera in an underwater housing, and lots of patience. Taking a picture underwater is a little more difficult than taking a picture on land. But after some practice you will soon be starting a photographic record of your skin diving experiences.

The camera you choose to take underwater with you does not have to be expensive or fancy. A simple underwater box camera will do nicely. These cameras are designed to go underwater just as they are.

Before you take one of these underwater cameras skin diving with you, check it in the bathtub for leaks. Watch for escaping air bubbles. If there are no bubbles, hold the camera at the bottom of the tub for at least three minutes. Then take it out of the water. Open the camera to see if there is any water in it. If any water has leaked in, you may need to put some silicone grease or petroleum jelly on the gasket. (The gasket generally looks like a fat, flat, rubber band. It is squeezed between the two sections of the camera to prevent water from leaking in.)

If fresh water gets into your underwater camera, wipe the inside of the camera with a soft, clean cloth. Then pour rubbing alcohol into the camera and swish it around. Pour the alcohol out. Any water left in the camera will mix with the alcohol. It will evaporate within minutes. Manipulate all the moving parts of the camera to be certain that water is not trapped in tiny crevices.

If salt water douses your camera during a day of skin diving, rinse it immediately with fresh water. Then use the alcohol as described before.

Do you own a simple box camera? You can take it underwater in a do-it-yourself watertight housing. The housing is easy to make. You will need a sturdy plastic bag (like the ones used to wrap fish purchased at a tropical fish store) and a skin diver's face mask. If the steel ring is held in place by screws, you will also need a pair of pliers and a screwdriver. When the ring is held by a simple clamp, no tools are needed.

Keep several plastic bags on hand as spares. Check all of them for leaks in the sink or bathtub. Inflate a bag, just like you blow air into a paper bag, and hold it underwater. If after several minutes no water leaks into the bag, it will keep your camera dry. Carefully dry the bags inside and out with a soft clean cloth.

The mask should have a safety glass face plate and a stainless steel ring. Remove the ring by taking the clamp off and then the glass. Handle the glass carefully. A scratch on the inside surface of the glass may be photographed and ruin your underwater pictures. Scratches on the outside surface are not so serious, but try to avoid them. Always clean the *inside* surface of the glass with a soft, clean cloth before you close the housing.

Make a final check to be sure that all the equipment is completely dry. Then put your camera inside the plastic bag. The camera lens should face the open end of the bag. (*Picture 31*) Now pull the open end of the bag through the mask—like threading a needle— and fold the ends back over the outside of the mask. (*Picture 32*) Allow about three inches of overlap. Put the glass face plate back into position. Be very careful. If you tear the bag you will have to start all over again. Clamp the ring back on the mask. It goes on top of the overlap of the plastic bag.

Test your underwater housing in the bathtub. (*Picture 33*) Pretend you are taking pictures. Practice working the camera controls through the plastic bag. Wait about ten minutes to be sure there are no leaks in your camera housing. None? Then it will be watertight from just beneath the surface down to a depth of about ten feet. Below that depth, the water pressure is too great for this type

Picture 31 Placing camera in plastic bag

Picture 32 Pulling bag through mask

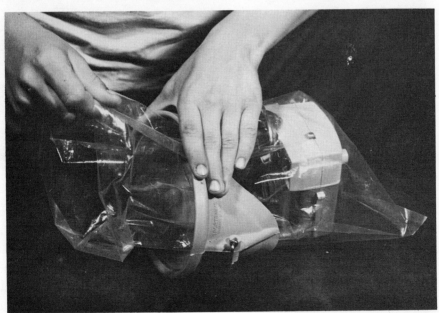

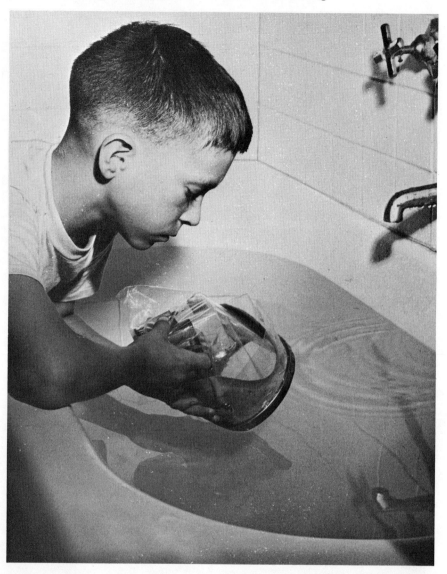

Picture 33 Testing underwater housing

of camera housing. But since your best pictures will be taken close to the surface, you will be a well-equipped underwater photographer.

It's best to start your underwater photography with black-and-white film, which is less expensive and easier to use than color film. Use Plus-X film if you are lucky enough to live near clear, bright water or if you can see approximately twenty feet underwater. You will need to use Tri-X film in most lakes and in northern salt water or where the visibility is less than fifteen feet. You can buy these films at your local drugstore. The temptation to use fancier, more expensive cameras and color film should be resisted, until you have some experience, and good results, with a simple camera and black-and-white film.

Light becomes less bright underwater. Some of the sun's rays bounce off the surface. The rays that go into the water are scattered in all directions by the millions of tiny particles suspended in the water. Fewer rays are bounced off the surface back into air when the sun is almost directly overhead, so that is the best time to take pictures underwater. But you can take pictures a few hours before and a few hours after with good results.

Rays of light are also bent when they pass from the air into the water. This bending causes everything underwater to appear one-fourth nearer to you than it actually is. Your eyes become used to this magnifying effect after a few days of diving.

Your best photographs will be the ones taken *near the surface* and *close to your subject*. Your camera-to-subject distance should not be more than one-fourth of the visibility. For instance, if the visibility is sixteen feet, your camera should not be more than four feet away from the subject you wish to photograph. The closer you get, the better the picture.

Be sure to hold the camera steady and to aim carefully when you snap a picture.

Don't expect to get professional-looking pictures on the very first day. It will take some time and patience to improve your underwater picture-taking technique. You will find lots of "models" to use for practice sessions. There are plenty of fish for you to photograph. If the fish won't pose for you, take pictures of your skin diving buddy.

What will your first pictures look like?

Everything in the picture blurred? Then you moved the camera. Hold the camera steady.

Subject is blurred but the background is not? Then the subject was moving too fast for your camera. You can get good pictures only if the motion is slower.

Two pictures in one? Then you forgot to wind your film. Get into the habit of winding the film just after you have taken a picture.

Picture too light? Then it is overexposed. Use a "slower" film. The clerk in the camera shop can help you to choose one.

Picture too dark? Then it is underexposed and you need a "faster" film.

Picture grayish with dark spots? Then your lens was dirty. Check the lens and the inside of your housing before each dive to make sure that they are clean. Use a tissue or soft cloth to wipe the dirt off.

Pictures perfect like these? (*Pictures 34, 35, 36, 37*) Then you are a top-notch underwater photographer!

Picture 34 Submerged wreck

Picture 35 A grouper

Picture 36 Gorgonian sea whips

Picture 37 Black angelfish

Whatever happens, don't get discouraged. Expect to make mistakes at first. After some practice, you will begin producing photographs that you will be proud to show to family and friends.

But please—don't get "carried away" by your underwater camera.

Don't forget to obey the skin diving safety rules while you are taking pictures underwater:

Dive with a buddy—he may want to take a camera along, too; or he can pose for you.

Use a diver's flag and surface float—you can carry your photo equipment in the float.

Wear a safety vest.

Wear a wet suit if the water is cold.

Check your weights in waist-high water before you dive.

Equalize your ears properly.

CHAPTER FIVE

Wildlife Underwater

Imagine that you and your buddy are snorkeling out to meet a special friend. The meeting place is not far from the sandy shore. You take breaths of air through your snorkels. Sure, smooth surface dives propel you toward the floor of the shallow lagoon. Visibility is good today. You can see clearly through your masks for almost fifty feet. Beyond this limit the view fades into a bluish haze. You hover over the submerged patchwork carpet: gently swaying sea moss, patches of sand, clumps of slippery rocks and beautiful coral. (*Picture 38*)

The underwater scenery is rippled with greenish-yellow sunlight and alive with tiny, busy fish. (*Picture 39*) A large dark fish turns tail abruptly and flees. A school of small silvery fish swarms by just over your heads. A lobster scutters to a hiding place. A startled scallop jet-propels itself out of sight. All around you there is a continuous hustle and bustle, accompanied by a chorus of beeps, snaps, and crackles.

You surface for air and dive again. Your friend finally arrives—late as usual, and cheerful as usual. Because his expression never changes from smiling, unfailing friendliness, you've nicknamed him Smiling Sam.

It is really a strange sort of friendship. Sam has never said a word to either you or your buddy. In fact, he doesn't speak the same language. You don't know how old he is, where he lives or even why he decided to befriend you. Your only means of communication is a mutual fondness for this wonderful, weightless un-

Picture 38 Sea moss, rocks, and coral

Picture 39 Pork fish

derwater world. And Sam's nimbleness underwater makes up for any social shortcomings. Sam can outswim and outmaneuver both of you. Next to Sam you feel awkward and ill-designed.

Sam joins you as, porpoiselike, you rise to the surface for air. You ask your camera-carrying buddy to take a picture of you and Sam together. The camera shutter clicks. Both of you want to prove to certain non-skin diving skeptics that such a fellow does exist. You offer Sam a small gift of friendship. You always bring him something. Sam graciously accepts the bit of food.

The photograph will show Sam's sleek, streamlined shape, his smooth, curved dorsal fin and his delightful, built-in grin. The photograph will prove—once and for all—that Sam is your friend. That a "wild" bottle-nosed dolphin knows and trusts you and welcomes your visits to his home. (*Picture 40*)

Imagine—a "wild" dolphin or fish for a friend!

Of course, a dolphin may never cross your underwater path, and

Picture 40 Bottle-nosed dolphin and friend

it will take patience and a slow, gentle manner to gain the confidence of any underwater animal. A "boyfish" like you may appear to be a strange and fearsome creature to fish. After all, a lot of people just want to catch them and eat them. You must give a fish time to get used to you and to realize that you mean no harm. It does take a while, but if you like animals of the sea as much as most skin divers do, you won't mind waiting.

Skin divers have made friends with bottle-nosed dolphins (probably the most popular marine animals in the world), groupers, angelfish, catfish, seals—the list is a long one.

If you meet a fish which doesn't swim away at the first sight of you but hangs around to see what you are up to, you might have the beginning of a very unusual friendship. Just take it slow and easy. Offer him food. And be very careful not to frighten him. You will be very proud if some day there is a fish in the ocean which regards you as a friend.

Of course, this kind of friendship is not limited to the ocean. It can happen in a river or a lake—anywhere you meet fish.

During your underwater travels you will see many different kinds of marine animals and plants. The underwater scenery is different in different parts of the oceans, just as scenery varies on land. And fesh-water displays are quite unlike salt water.

Tropical waters are much different from northern waters. Everything is more colorful as you venture south. In southern waters you find coral reefs which range in color from a reddish-brown to brilliant orange. The fish which live among the coral reefs are usually more richly colored than the somber-toned fish of the north.

While skin diving around a coral reef you are likely to see pretty blue parrot fish (*Picture 41*), bright yellow grunts, vivid yellow queen triggerfish trimmed with blue (*Picture 42*), black angelfish with clownish, chalk-white mouths, and curious, boldly striped sergeant majors. (*Picture 43*)

You will see these and other colorful fish swimming among many kinds of coral. You might see tiny sea polyps that look like tiny Christmas trees nestled snugly on a large brain coral—so called because it resembles a brain (*Picture 44*). Small fish find shelter in a forest of staghorn coral (*Picture 45*). Nearby and all around there

Picture 41
Blue parrot fish

Picture 42
Queen triggerfish

Picture 43
Boldly striped
sergeant majors

Picture 44 Brain coral

Picture 45 Staghorn coral

may be delicate, purplish sea fans swaying with the current. Beyond all this you may see majestic antler coral. (*Picture 46*)

There are also many kinds of sponges living on the ocean floor. Perhaps you will see a colonial vase sponge which you can recognize by the large holes. A fish might be seen "resting" in a big basket sponge. (*Picture 47*)

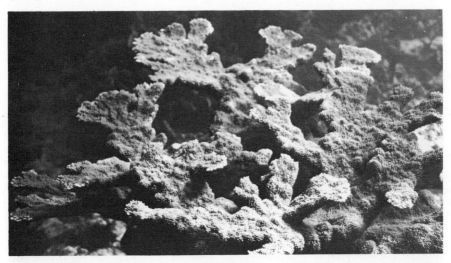

Picture 46 Antler coral

Picture 47 Fish in a basket sponge

Sea anemones are fascinating animals which look like flowers. (*Picture 48*) Their color ranges from bright green, soft blues and reds to stark black and white. These unusual animals just sit and wait for some unlucky tiny fish to swim into their petal-like tentacles. You will find them on sunken ships in northern waters as well as on coral reefs in Florida waters.

Picture 48 Sea anemones

Then, of course, there are starfish, sand dollars, crabs, lobsters, shrimp, oysters, scallops, and many other varieties of marine life.

Now all of these are attractive, interesting to watch, and harmless. But, as in any community of wildlife, there are certain marine animals which can be harmful to you. Here are some of these "bad guys" in a

SALT WATER ROGUES GALLERY

Fire coral is easy to recognize. Although it grows in different forms, it is always a mustard-yellow color and has a smooth surface. (*Picture 49*) (Other coral has a rough surface with a lot of little

Picture 49 Fire coral

pores in it.) If you touch fire coral—or are brushed against it by a current—you will feel just the same as if you had been burned by a hot iron. The injured place on your leg or arm will turn red and hurt for an hour or so. Then it will turn white and sting awhile longer. Gradually it will stop hurting. Naturally, it is better to be careful and not get "burned" in the first place.

Spiny sea urchins look like large pin cushions holding hundreds of long sharp needles. (*Picture 50*) They sit quietly on the ocean bottom nestled around rocks and coral. They can only move slowly on tiny tube feet. It is up to you to look out for them. If you step on

Picture 50 Spiny sea urchins

a sea urchin or try to pick it up you are certain to get a giant needle in your foot or hand. The brittle needle will break off at the skin surface. And there you are—with a big black needle that stings like the dickens. All you can do is put some antiseptic on the wound and wait for the needle to dissolve in your skin.

Sting rays look like huge dark butterflies when you see them swimming gracefully through the water. (*Picture 51*) They will not attack you. In fact, they will swim away from you. You can watch

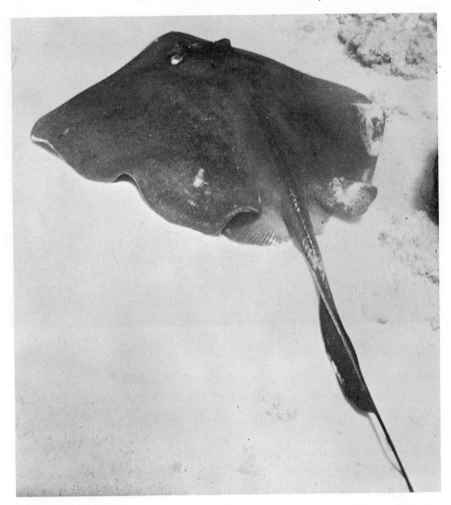

Picture 51 Sting ray

them or photograph them as much as you please. Just be careful not to step on one that is lying peacefully on the bottom. Who can blame a stepped-on sting ray for defending itself? The large stinger is near the base of the ray's tail and can cause a very painful injury.

Jellyfish appear in great numbers at certain times of the year. (*Picture 52*) There are many different kinds—most of them are pretty to look at, but some can inflict a severe sting. Jellyfish move through

Picture 52 Jellyfish

the water by opening and closing their umbrellas. They move quietly and a lot faster than you might think they could. If you see one moving in your direction, give him the right of way!

Portuguese man-of-war is one of the most powerful stingers because of its large size. (*Picture 53*) It grows to as much as a foot across the float with tentacles that may be as long as thirty feet. You have to watch out for them. The Portuguese man-of-war is usually seen sailing along on the surface with its long tentacles trailing below in the water. Since it is going where the wind and the current takes it, *you* have to get out of *its* way. Sometimes, as in rough or stormy weather, the man-of-war deflates its gas-filled float and goes underwater.

What happens if you don't see a Portuguese man-of-war or a stinging jellyfish and you don't dodge out of its way in time? If you are wearing a wet suit it will protect you from stings. If not, you will get stung. And it hurts. First, rub all the tentacles off your skin with sand or a towel. Douse the area with diluted ammonia

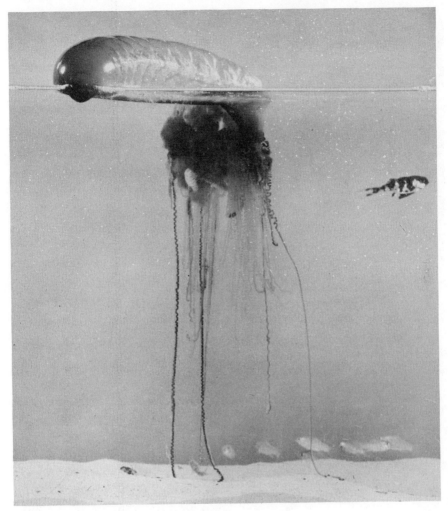

Picture 53 Portuguese man-of-war

or alcohol or gasoline. Then use a soothing lotion to relieve the stinging. If you ran into a big one and feel sick, *go to a doctor right away*.

One more word of caution—the Portuguese man-of-war and jellyfish are sometimes washed up on the beach. They may appear to be dead, but they can still sting you. Don't handle them.

Moray eels are usually found in their favorite homes—nice dark holes in a coral reef or under a rock—with just their heads stick-

Picture 54 Moray eel

ing out. (*Picture 54*) A moray eel won't come dashing out of its home and attack you. But he will regard you as an enemy if you disturb him by poking a stick or your hand into his home. Then he will come out to defend himself. The moray eel has very strong jaws equipped with very sharp teeth and can hurt you very badly. It is foolish to tease or disturb him. Leave him alone and he won't bother you.

Barracuda look very mean. (*Picture 55*) Actually, like the moray eel, they will not harm you if you don't frighten or harm them. However, they are attracted by bright, shiny objects. Don't wear a shiny

Picture 55 Barracuda

watch, ring, etc., when skin diving in waters where barracuda are generally seen. Barracuda are very curious. They will sometimes follow along behind you. If this bothers you, just turn around and face them and they will swim away from you.

Sharks are feared by some people and laughed at by others. (*Picture 56*) No one really knows very much about sharks. Studies are being made by a Shark Research panel. This panel is sponsored by the Biology Branch of the Office of Naval Research and the Smithsonian Institution.

Picture 56 Shark

As far as anyone knows right now, sharks are not very intelligent. They seem to pick up vibrations in the water, such as those caused by a wounded, struggling fish. They seem to have a keen sense of smell and they seem to have much better eyesight than they are generally given credit for. It will probably be quite some time before anyone knows exactly why sharks behave the way they do.

But we do know this much: some sharks are big, have large mouths and jagged teeth, can move fast, and therefore can be dangerous. A shark might not *mean* to do you any harm at all, but it *might* mistake you for a sick or wounded fish—which is part of its diet. It is not sensible to take a chance.

If you see a shark—and the odds are less than one in several thousand that you will—just don't give it a chance to mistake you for something else. Get out of the water right away. Get into the boat, or swim slowly to shore—always keeping your eye on the shark. Never turn your back on the shark. Just as an untamed donkey might charge you if your back is turned, a shark might charge. Most wild or untamed animals, and marine animals included, seem reluctant to attack a person who is facing them.

Please never try to ride on a shark's back, or pull his tail, or try to stick him with a knife or spear. The shark certainly won't like you for it, and could very well be provoked into biting you.

There is one important thing for skin divers to remember. Most animals in the sea eat early in the morning and again just when it begins to grow dark. You should stay on your own "home ground" at these times. Leave the sea to the sea creatures at dawn and at dusk—when the sea becomes a hungry jungle. Each animal, large or small, is out looking for something to eat. They are not smart enough to know that you are not just another tasty fish to add to their menu.

Water snakes, of various sizes and coloring, may be found in and near many bodies of fresh water. However, there is only one venomous species, the water moccasin or "cottonmouth," which lives only in the Southern states. It can be distinguished from other, non-venomous, snakes by the two deep pits between the eyes and nostrils and by its large, stout body. (*Picture 57*) Water snakes will generally go out of their way to avoid you. But if you block a snake's avenue of escape or molest it, it will, quite naturally, defend itself.

Whether you dive in salt water or fresh water, stay away from any thickly grown underwater plants longer than three feet. A skin diver simply does not have enough air to spend time getting untangled.

Learn to identify the various kinds of fish in your diving area. Then you can recognize and avoid contact with any fish which may be harmful. Some fish have one or more sharp spines on their fins. For example, the catfish, in both salt and fresh water, has such a

Picture 57 Water moccasin snake

weapon on each pectoral fin (the fin just behind the gills); sometimes it also has a spine on the dorsal fin (the high fin on its back). (*Picture 58*)

Picture 58 Catfish

And, finally, don't dive in stagnant or polluted water. Unhealthy bodies of water may cause uncomfortable skin infections or otherwise mar your own good health.

Use caution. Don't try to be a "hero," and you will have many years of underwater enjoyment and exploration ahead of you.

The sea covers about 70 per cent of the earth's surface. Five-sixths of the living matter that exists on earth is found in the sea. There is much to be seen and much to be learned.

You can hope to have a fish-friend someday. You can look forward to the day you meet a bottle-nosed dolphin, that friendly and well-loved mammal. You can spend your skin diving days diving just for the fun of it. Or—as many scientists hope—you can spend at least part of your diving time gathering information about underwater life, information which will help us to understand our neighbors who live beneath the surface.

Whenever you go skin diving, please remember that you are a visitor in the underwater world. When you visit someone's home you certainly do not break the furniture and kick the dog. When you visit the water world remember your good manners—don't destroy plants and coral or molest the animals.

Here are a few rules for your safety:

Never molest any underwater animal
Look around you . . . avoid swimming into or stepping on jellyfish, Portuguese man-of-war, sea urchins, and sting rays
Stay away from fire coral
Leave the water if you see a shark
Never turn your back on a shark
Don't touch spiny fish
Never swim in thick plant beds more than three feet long
Don't dive in stagnant or polluted water

CHAPTER SIX

Fish for Your Supper

Spearfishing can be a useful addition to your skin diving skills, but you will not be a good sportsman if you use your underwater weapon to kill fish just for the fun of it. A good rule to follow is: *spear a fish only if you intend to eat it.*

The rubber-powered handspear is of simple one-piece construction and the safest of all the underwater weapons. (*Picture 59*) It has a fiber glass shaft which is from four to eight feet long. The four- or six-foot size will be best for you.

The handspear or sealance has a rubber sling which propels the shaft. Stretch the rubber by moving your hand forward along the shaft. Keep a firm grip on the shaft. Hold the rubber between your thumb and first finger. (*Picture 60*) Aim and release the shaft, but keep hold of the rubber sling. Then take your speared fish to shore, boat, or watertight float.

The handspear, besides being the safest underwater weapon, is also the most sportsmanlike weapon. However, you may want to try one of the more powerful spearguns which you will see displayed in the dive shop. *Please try only the junior guns.* The adult-sized guns are too big and too powerful for you to handle safely.

The junior arbalete (*Picture 61*) is one of the small guns which you may safely use *if you learn to use it properly under adult supervision,* and use it *only* when accompanied by an experienced adult spearfisherman. It looks like a long pistol and has rubber tubing at the "business end," a separate spear, and a trigger safety. *Keep the safety mechanism on until you are ready to shoot.*

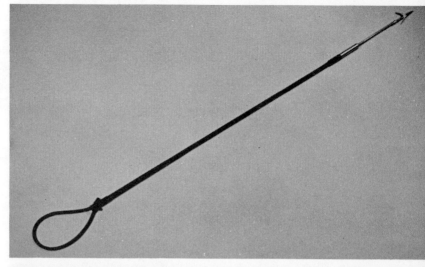

Picture 59
The rubber-
powered
handspear

Picture 60
Proper way
to stretch
rubber sling

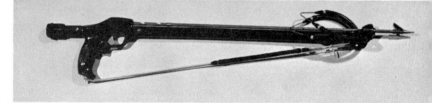

Picture 61
The junior
arbalete

Always load your speargun *underwater*. You must never load a speargun on the beach, in a boat, or on a surface float. A shaft released in air can cause fatal injury to an innocent bystander. A shaft carelessly fired underwater may injure another diver. (If you find that a powered speargun is too difficult for you to handle underwater, then stick with the handspear until you are older and stronger.)

It takes time and a lot of practice to learn to use your handspear or speargun skillfully and safely. You should get some target practice before you begin to spear fish. Use something soft for your underwater target so you don't damage the spearhead. An old burlap bag will do nicely.

When you start out to hunt for your supper, keep your spear pointed *down* and *away* from your diving buddy. Snorkel *quietly* along the surface. A lot of splashing on the surface will frighten fish away. Tow a watertight surface float with a diver's flag attached. An inner tube stretched around a washtub makes a good float for spearfishermen, because the leakproof tub can be used to hold your catch.

Tie a nylon line (see Chapter One) to the float. Either you or your non-spearfishing buddy can tow the float and flag along with you. You can attach the line to a very stong rubber band and slip the rubber band on to your wrist. Then you can tow the float and flag, and still have both hands free to hunt. (*Picture 62*)

Picture 62
Using a line
and float

Make very quiet surface dives to explore the area. Look around rocks, wrecks, coral reefs—any place where a fish might hide. (*Pictures 63, 64*) When you see your "supper" get as close as you can without alarming the fish, swimming smoothly and slowly. Practice will help you to allow for refraction and currents when you aim. Aim just behind the gills. (*Picture 65*)

Picture 63 Exploring underwater

Picture 64 Fish hiding here?

Picture 65 Aim just behind the gills

Once you spear a fish, get it out of the water and into the float right away! *Don't hang speared fish around your waist.* Some divers who have done that have learned better the hard way. Their fish have been taken away from them by big and very hungry sharks.

Make the sharks hunt for their own supper. Once you have your meal on the spear, put it in the float and take it back to the boat or to shore so that you can eat it yourself!

Care of Spearfishing Equipment: Always rinse your speargun in fresh water after using it in salt water. Lubricate the arbalete trigger mechanism with a light coat of oil. (Heavy grease will pick up sand and grit.) Wipe all metal parts lightly with oil, being careful not to get oil on the rubber strands. The rubber should be powdered with the same special powder you use for your wet suit.

Inspect the rubber strands *before* each dive. If the strands look worn or the rubber is cracked it is no longer safe to use. It may snap back and break your mask. Have the strands replaced before you use the speargun again. Don't spear just any fish that happens to come within range of your speargun. Some fish are good eating, but some are poisonous and should never be eaten. Find out which fish are good to eat in your hunting area, and know how to identify them. You can get this information by writing to your State Fisheries Bureau or the United States Fish and Wildlife Service, or ask your biology teacher for local information.

There are laws concerning the spearing of fish. In some areas it is against the law to spear *any* fish. In other areas only certain fish can be speared. Be sure to find out what the laws are in your particular area.

Perhaps you think that success with a speargun is all a spearfisherman needs. That is not the case. A *successful* spearfisherman is the one who not only provides the meal but also cooks the day's catch to perfection. So take off those gloves and prepare for the

SPEARFISHERMAN'S LAMENT or
HOW TO CLEAN AND COOK FISH

First, scrape the fish from the tail toward the head, to remove the scales. Use the back of a knife. Hold the knife nearly flat against the fish. Make a slit from the gills to the vent (*Picture 66*) and remove the innards. Cut off the head (including the gills) and the tail. Now wash the fish thoroughly.

Picture 66 Make a slit from gills to vent

Skin fish: To skin a fish, first remove the fins along the backbone. (*Picture 67*) Cut off a narrow strip of skin along the entire length of the backbone. Pull the skin off toward the tail. Remove the skin from one side of the fish and then turn the fish over and do the other side. (*Picture 68*)

Picture 67 Remove fins along the backbone

Picture 68 Pull skin off toward the tail

Bone fish: Cut the backbone away from the flesh on one side, beginning at the tail. Then do the same on the other side of the backbone. Now take out the backbone and any small bones. Spread the fish open in one piece. Now you have a filet. (A piece of fish without skin and bones is called a filet.) You can fry, bake, broil, or boil a filet.

Fish bake: If you like, you can take your fish home and cook it on the stove. But if you want to be a *real* outdoorsman, cook it over an open fire right on the beach. A fish bake is the perfect way to end a day of skin diving and spearfishing. As the sun goes down, the salt air becomes a bit chilly, so a fire is in order. Everyone is hungry. Why not cook your fish then and there?

To cook a truly delicious fish over an open fire you need a little butter, a lemon, and salt and pepper. Brush the fish with butter. Give it a sprinkling of salt and pepper. Squeeze the lemon juice over the fish. Wrap the fish in aluminum foil. Now put it over a charcoal fire for about fifteen minutes on each side.

When you are spearfishing it is very important that you remember the skin diving safety rules as well as the following spearfishing safety rules:

Handle your underwater weapon with great care

Never point a speargun at anyone on the beach or underwater

Be absolutely sure you are aiming at a fish before you release the shaft

Always remove the spearhead out of the water

Never load a speargun on the beach

Always load your speargun underwater

Always keep the safety mechanism on until you are ready to shoot

Take proper care of your speargun

Inspect the rubber strands before each dive

Get speared fish out of the water right away

Never tie speared fish around your waist

Never spear a fish you do not intend to eat

Always be sure the fish you spear are edible

Wear gloves when handling lobsters and crabs

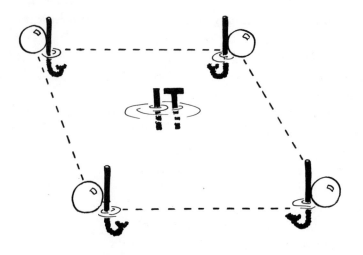

Picture 69 Musical snorkels

CHAPTER SEVEN

Fun and Games Underwater

What could be better on a hot summer day than a skin diving party? These games can be played in a pool or in clear, shallow water, in a river, lake, or the ocean—always under the supervision of an adult, of course. The games can be played just for fun or, if it is an honest-to-goodness party, for prizes.

Musical Snorkels: Attach a balloon or some other small flotation device to each of four snorkels. Then place the snorkels in the water at equal distances to form a fifteen-foot square. Now, station four divers at the four snorkels floating on the surface. The four divers keep their heads underwater and breathe through the snorkels. One diver, without a snorkel, is stationed at the center of the square. (To be fair, this should be you.) (*Picture 69*)

The four divers must try to switch snorkels without raising their heads above water. They can swim underwater in any direction, but they must leave the snorkels floating in place behind them. The diver in the center, who is IT, must try to capture an empty snorkel. If IT gets to a snorkel first, he claims it. The diver who finds himself without a snorkel becomes IT.

Capture the Flag: Draw lots among the divers to form two teams. Give each diver a square of cloth, such as a handkerchief or a rag, to tuck into the side of his bathing suit.

Divide the pool, or in open water a square about twenty feet, lengthwise by a weighted line. The line can be a clothesline held

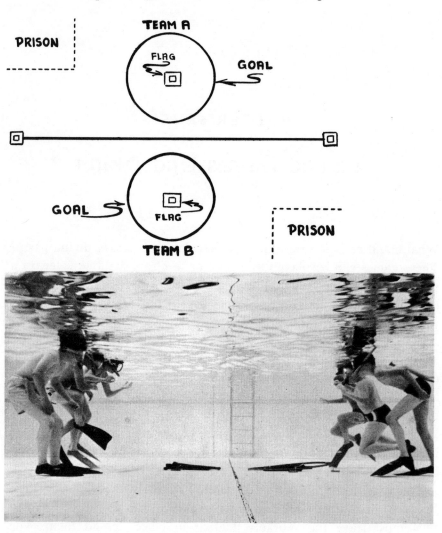

Picture 70 Ready to "Capture the Flag"

down under the water with stones or lead weights. Place one weighted hula hoop about two feet beyond the line on each side. These represent the goal areas. Put a small (one pound) lead weight or a fin inside each hula hoop. These are the "flags." (*Picture 70*)

Now, Team A members must swim underwater to capture Team B's flag and vice versa. But if an A man goes into B's territory and a B man captures his cloth (*Picture 71*), the A man must go to

Picture 71 A prisoner!

prison on the surface in the corner of B's territory. Then he can be freed from prison only if touched by a teammate. The same thing happens to a B man in A's territory.

The game is played until one team captures the other team's flag, or until everyone on one team goes to prison.

Snatch the Bacon: To play this game, you need a referee and two teams. Station the teams on opposite sides of the pool, or on either side of a marked-off area in open water. Each diver on a team is given a number. The divers on the second team are given the *same* numbers.

The "bacon" is placed dead center on the bottom of the pool or marked-off area. The bacon can be a small (one pound) lead weight from a weight belt or it can be a fin.

The referee calls a number. The two divers with that number surface dive and try to snatch the bacon and swim back to their own side without being tagged. (*Picture 72*) If a diver is successful, his team gets three points. If he is tagged by the other diver, he must give the bacon to his opponent who then makes one point for his team.

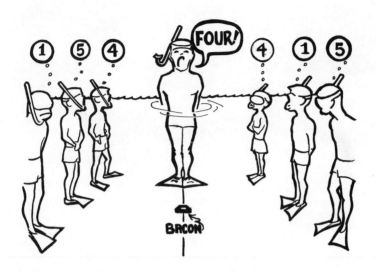

Picture 72 Playing Snatch the Bacon

Underwater Obstacle Course: Weighted hula hoops can be used to set up an underwater obstacle course. (*Picture 73*) Draw a chart showing the divers where to begin the course, where to surface for air, and where to finish. Set a reasonable time limit for running the course. The diver who swims the course correctly and closest to the allowed time is the winner.

Picture 73 Swimming through an underwater obstacle

Red Rover: Stretch two weighted lines across the bottom of the pool, about fifteen feet apart. All the divers, except the one chosen to be IT, stay behind one of the lines.

IT stays in the center area. He calls a diver by saying, "Red Rover, Red Rover, let —— come over." The diver called must surface dive and try to swim underwater to the other line without being caught by IT. (*Picture 74*) If he succeeds, he is safe. But if he is caught, he must stay in the center area and help IT catch the other divers who are called. This can be played until finally all the divers are caught. The last diver caught becomes IT.

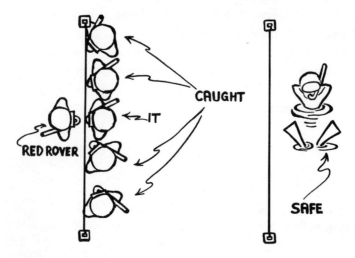

Picture 74 Playing Red Rover

Follow the Leader: Draw lots to choose the leader. In a pool or open water (in open water the boundaries must be set by an adult supervising diver) the leader does his best to lose his followers. He somersaults, stands on his head and floats feet-first to the surface, and so on. The diver who fails to keep up with the leader must then take the lead.

Treasure Hunt: Shiny objects, such as spoons and marbles, are placed on the bottom of the pool or in open water. A small plastic slate is attached to each object. A clue is written on each plastic slate which leads to the next clue and finally to the treasure. The diver who finds the treasure is the winner and keeps the prize. (Hard-boiled eggs can be used for an underwater Easter egg hunt.)

Commercial Games: When you shop for your skin diving equipment, you will probably see one or two underwater games on the shelf. These are games designed by experienced divers to add to your underwater fun.

One such game provides harmless copies of the Hawaiian Sling speargun and an underwater target to test the diver's skill and aim. This is a good skin diving party game.

How to Make Pin Money Underwater: Would you like to make a little money using your skin diving skills? Do you live near a golf course? Or a boat marina? Or a fishermen's favorite stream? If so, you are probably in business.

Inquire at the golf course. How many golf balls have been lost in water traps? You and your buddy offer to recover them for a reasonable price. Do the job well and perhaps you will have a permanent client.

Inquire at the marina. Has anyone lost a boat mooring? Or a *small* anchor in *shallow* water?

Offer to look for the fisherman's lost rod and reel in his favorite stream.

In fact, any time you hear of a *small* object lost in *shallow* water, you have a chance to become a "professional" diver. Of course, it can't be anything too big and too heavy for you to bring to the surface. And you won't always find what you are looking for. But it is worth a try.

And remember these safety rules:

Games must always be supervised by an adult diver
In open water, boundaries must be set by an adult diver
Always dive with a buddy
Offer to recover only small objects in shallow water

CHAPTER EIGHT

Hobbies for the Skin Diver

Exploring the underwater world is like visiting another planet. You will feel almost weightless—as if you had left earth's gravity far behind you. It is a colorful world. But the colors are soft like a pastel picture. It is a wilderness filled with animals of all sizes and shapes. They range in size from animals as large as a truck to those that are tinier than a pin point. Some marine animals are sleek and beautiful. Some are weird. Some are comical. You will find a busy, restless world in constant motion beneath the surface. It is unlike anything you have ever experienced on land.

It is not surprising that most skin divers want more than a memory to tide them over until the next day of diving. A pretty shell is picked up and displayed at home. Then another shell and perhaps a broken piece of coral. This is the beginning of an underwater hobby. The water world is full to the brim with hobby possibilities. Here are a few suggestions which may interest you:

Salt-Water Aquarium: Fresh-water aquariums have been popular for many years. A salt-water or marine aquarium is much more difficult to take care of. But it can be done. Just be sure to get all the expert advice you can before you start on such a project. Here are a few hints to get you started:

First, remember that salt-water fish are delicate. Be very gentle with them. Fish have a slippery protective coating on their bodies. If this coating is rubbed off by too much handling, the fish will become sick and probably die. It is important that fish be handled as little as possible.

Equipment for Collecting Fish (*Picture 75*)

  Net, with handle
  Plastic bags and rubber bands
  Small portable foam-plastic ice box
  Lots of patience

Picture 75 Equipment for collecting fish

Collecting Fish: Look for small, brightly colored fish. *Do not destroy fishes' homes by breaking coral and overturning rocks. If you lift a rock during your search, be sure to put it back exactly where you found it.*

When you see a small fish you would like to care for in your home, hold the net so that it flows out with the current. With a little luck, careful maneuvering, and the aid of the current, the fish will land in the net. Then transfer the fish from the net into the plastic bag—*underwater*. It is possible that the fish may be frightened by the net and will be caught more easily by the "invisible" plastic bag. Take the plastic bag onto the boat or shore. Never take the fish out of the water. The fish must remain in its "home" water—the same water in which it was caught.

Fish cannot live in overheated water. The foam plastic container will keep the water from overheating until you reach home. Put the plastic bag (which you can get from your local tropical fish store) inside the foam plastic container. The bag should hold about four inches of the "home" water as well as the small captive fish. Wind the top of the bag. Seal the top with a rubber band. (*Picture 76*) The space in the bag above the water is filled with air. Now your fish should be able to travel comfortably from its old home to its new home, the aquarium.

The new home must be carefully prepared *weeks* in *advance* of the fish's arrival. The water must be properly "cured." And any and all shells or coral must be sterile before being put into the aquarium.

Collecting Coral: Look for coral that has been broken by storms or anchors. You need only small pieces for your aquarium. Again, please do not break up the living coral as it provides food and shelter for marine life.

Perhaps there is no coral in your diving area. (The only living coral reefs off the North American coasts are found in the Florida waters.) You will find small pieces of coral suitable for your aquarium on sale at your tropical fish store.

Coral is actually a mass of thousands of tiny skeletons of thousands of tiny animals. These animals have protective skeletons outside their bodies instead of inside their bodies as we do. The shells

Picture 76 Carrying fish in his "home" water

you find were also hard protective coats for small animals. You must be sure that there is no decayed matter from little dead animals trapped inside the coral or shells. They must be absolutely clean and sterile before being put into the aquarium. Decayed matter will release poisonous gases into the aquarium and may cause your hard-won fish to die.

Soak all the pieces in fresh water for two to three weeks. Change the water every other day. Give the pieces one final fresh-water rinse at the end of that time.

Now the coral and shells should have no decaying odor. They should smell fresh and clean. Place them in the sun to dry. Use the same treatment for coral you collect yourself and the coral you buy from the store.

Setting up the Aquarium: Glass or clear plastic aquariums provide the safest homes for your marine animals. Neither of these requires cement which may become poisonous to the fish when it comes into contact with salt water. And since these do not have metal frames, there is no danger of rust or corrosion.

You will need a flat piece of plastic which has small holes or slots in it. This is a subsand filter. It acts as a false bottom in your aquarium. The subsand filter prevents stagnation by allowing the water to circulate under the sand.

With the addition of a small air pump you will be able to keep your aquarium clean and clear for months at a time.

You must "cure" your aquarium, the subsand filter, and any additional equipment that will be used in the tank. Fill the tank with fresh water. Add three tablespoons of table salt for each gallon of water. Let the aquarium sit for several days. Then siphon off the salted water and rinse all equipment with fresh water. Fill the tank again with fresh water and empty it once more.

You can use the commercial aquarium gravel in your salt-water tank, but it must be properly cleaned. Put the gravel in a clean enamel bucket. Fill the bucket with fresh water. Stir the gravel for several minutes and pour the water off. Keep doing this until the water looks clear and clean. Then the gravel is ready to be put into the aquarium.

Decide where you want to display your salt-water aquarium. It should be placed where there are no drafts, and where it will receive about an hour of sunlight each morning and late afternoon.

Put about an inch of gravel on top of the subsand filter. Then add one or two of the nicest pieces of coral to provide hiding places for your fish. (*Picture 77*) Perhaps you have a shell which will make

Picture 77 Salt-water aquarium

a snug home for a tiny fish. Give each piece of coral and each shell one last sniff test before placing it in your aquarium. If any piece has the slightest unpleasant odor, it is not properly cured. It must go back into fresh water for another week or longer.

Now you can fill the aquarium with water. But it must be either fresh—and pure—sea water or artificial sea water from the tropical fish store. Turn on the air pump. The aquarium is ready at last. You can begin your search for a few small hearty tenants—just put on your mask, fins, and snorkel.

Decorating Starfish: Starfish have made themselves very unpopular. They like to eat oysters. Thousands of hungry starfish have gobbled up oysters at such a rate that they have become a real nuisance. In the past there have been "star mops." Skin divers were asked to dive for as many starfish as possible. So the divers "mopped" up starfish by the thousands. Most of these were destroyed.

But why let mopped-up starfish go to waste? They can be used in many ways, to make unusual and thoughtful gifts.

Collecting: Equipment: cloth bag and gloves. All you do is dive to the bottom, pick up the starfish, and put it in the bag. They do not bite or sting.

Curing: Some divers just put the starfish out to dry in the sun for a day or two. These starfish last quite a while but they may become a bit brittle.

Starfish will last indefinitely if you:

Dry them in the sun

Soak them in 70% alcohol for one month

Dry them in the sun again

Decorating: Supplies: glue, glitter, fake jewels, and anything else you can think of. You can find the hardware necessary to make jewelry in a hobby shop. The decorating is really up to you. Use your imagination. Experiment with new ideas. Here are a few suggestions. (*Picture 78*)

Tiny starfish painted with bright metallic gold or silver paint— found in an artist's supply store—can be made into sparkling earrings or pins.

Use the handy spray-enamel paints and string "stars" of several lively colors to make a bracelet or necklace.

You can make an attractive ring for Mom. Color a tiny star. Glue a small make-believe pearl on it. Then glue the star to a plain ring band.

How about cuff links and a tiepin for Dad?

Tiny starfish, seahorses, sea shells, etc., imbedded in clear plastic make useful and unusual paperweights and penholders. Small underwater creatures can be preserved in a large shell. The molds and ingredients for mixing the clear plastic are available at hobby shops. Ask your dad to help you mix the chemicals to be sure it is done properly and safely.

Picture 78 Decorating ideas

One or two old wire clothes hangers, some thin picture-hanging wire, and decorated starfish, shells, etc., can be fashioned into a handsome mobile. (*Picture 79*)

Dressed-up "stars" can be added to your Christmas decorations. (*Picture 80*) Cover the upper side of the starfish with glue. Then sprinkle red, blue, or silver glitter over it. On another star—use a tube of household cement to make a thin outline around the "arms." Then sprinkle colored glitter over the glue. You can use several colors. Attach big pretend diamonds, pearls, or rubies to the starfish and color around them. Any of these—when hung on a crisp, green tree—will sparkle and twinkle like stars among the Christmas tree lights.

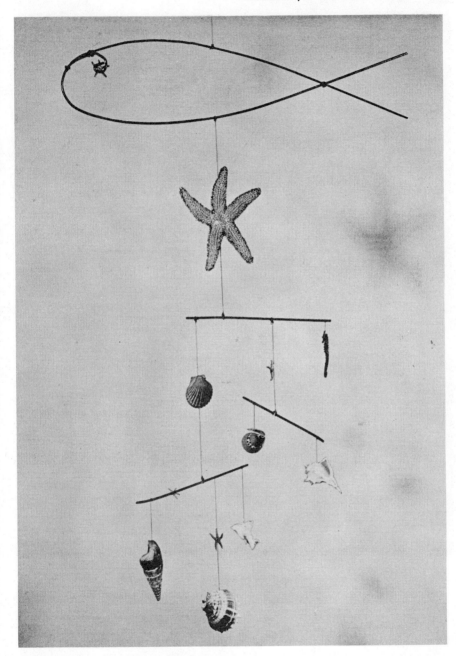

Picture 79 An easy-to-make mobile

Picture 80 Starfish as Christmas decorations

Try making a Santa Claus using red glitter and fluffy white cotton. Make an angel with silver wings and a dainty silver halo. You can make decorations for the entire Christmas tree.

Do you have a basket sponge? Fill it with shiny Christmas balls. Pin a brightly colored star on it and add it to your holiday decorations.

How to Make Shell Pictures:

   Supplies: Lots of shells . . . all shapes and sizes and colors

   Bits of coral and tiny starfish

   A board or panel canvas

   Glue and wire

   Paints and imagination

   Collect the shells and bits of coral, tiny starfish—anything you come across while diving.

   If you feel ambitious, paint an underwater scene on the canvas. Make the shells, coral, and starfish part of the scene. Or paint the background a solid color. Then use your collection to make an attractive and colorful design. You can either glue or wire the materials in place. Put a frame on your finished picture. Hang it on your wall—or give it as a gift to Mom, Dad, or a special friend. (*Picture 81*)

Picture 81 A lovely shell picture

Fish Prints:

Supplies: Fish you have speared for supper

Several straight pins (from your mother's sewing box)

India ink

Red sable brush about ½ inch wide

Rice paper

Sheet of cardboard (all found in an artist's supply store)

This is a simple, yet permanent, way to keep a record of the fish you catch for supper. Make a fish print right on the spot.

Pin the fish by the fins to the piece of cardboard. (*Picture 82*) Let the fish dry out in the sun for several minutes. When it seems nearly dry—brush lightly over the entire fish with the India ink. Brush from back to front. If you work quickly and carefully, you can use two or more colors. (*Picture 83*) Very carefully smooth the rice paper over the entire fish. (*Picture 84*) Let the paper sit for a few minutes—until the ink is dry. Now slowly pull the rice paper off the fish. The print you hold in your hand will last for your lifetime. (*Picture 85*) Frame it and hang it on your wall. Now you have your fish and can eat it too!

Picture 82 Pin fish to cardboard

Picture 83 Brush ink on from back to front

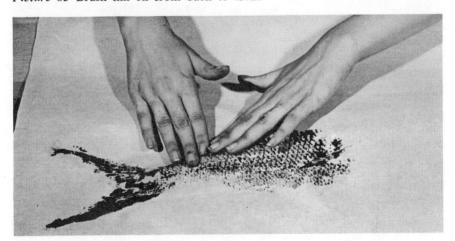

Picture 84 Smooth rice paper over entire fish

Picture 85 The finished print

CHAPTER NINE

Undersea Science

"Knowledge of the oceans is more than a matter of curiosity. Our very survival may hinge on it."
President John Fitzgerald Kennedy
Message to Congress, 1961

Today the biggest, most unexplored, most challenging wilderness on earth is beneath the sea. Until just a few years ago, underwater exploration was difficult and limited to few people. But now, with the help of modern skin diving and compressed-air diving equipment, all divers who wish to be can be pioneers—pioneers in gathering facts about the underwater world. Any new knowledge that skin divers can contribute is important to scientists, for very little is known about day-to-day marine life. What do fish do all day? How does one fish get along with other fish? What do they eat? Where do they find shelter from their enemies? What kinds of marine life, other than fish, can provide food for the world's growing population?

Some divers thoughtlessly and needlessly destroy the homes and lives of marine plants and animals, not intentionally but because they lack adequate knowledge. To help prevent this destruction, the American Littoral Society was organized to interest the ever-increasing numbers of skin divers in the *study* and *protection* of marine life.

Perhaps you will become interested in doing useful work with your skin diving ability. Perhaps you will want to explore and observe the wilderness beneath the surface—and contribute vital information about marine life. You will add a whole new dimension to your diving but, in turn, you will have a lot to learn: how to identify the many marine plants and animals, and how to report accurately what you have observed—the locality, the water depth, the name of the species, its size, weight, and so on.

The American Littoral Society is organizing a Junior Division for boys and girls like you. Within this division, a Marine Biology Summer Camp under the direction of Mr. Buster Crabbe and Mr. Jim Cahill was started in the summer of 1963. Students who have not already learned to skin dive are taught the necessary skin diving skills at camp. All students learn to properly identify the numerous marine animals found in the shallow water along the camp's beachfront. Before long, they are off on skin diving "field" trips in clear, shallow water to observe underwater life and to collect a few specimens for further study.

Plans are being made for a high school marine biology-skin diving program. There is also an Explorer Scout program for boys fourteen years and up who are interested in marine biology. Although it is connected with the Boy Scouts of America, it is not necessary to be a Boy Scout member.

For information about any of these programs write to: Junior Division, American Littoral Society, Highlands, New Jersey

What about the future? Your generation will produce young scientists and technicians to carry on the study of the sea. Perhaps your skin diving skills and your interest in the sea will lead you to one of the many phases of underwater research.

Perhaps you will become interested in marine biology, the science which deals with the origin, history, physical characteristics, and habits of marine plants and animals.

Pretend that, right now, you are a marine biologist. You are studying the possibility of future undersea farms. These farms may be the only way to produce enough food, fish, and sea plants to feed our expanding population in years to come.

What is your working day, as a marine biologist, like? You use skin diving and compressed-air diving equipment to chart a small, shallow area of the ocean floor. The large chart when completed will show which parts of the charted area are mostly sand, grass, coral, or mud. (*Picture 86*) When this is done, you put colored tags, using a different color for each section, on some of the animals so that you can

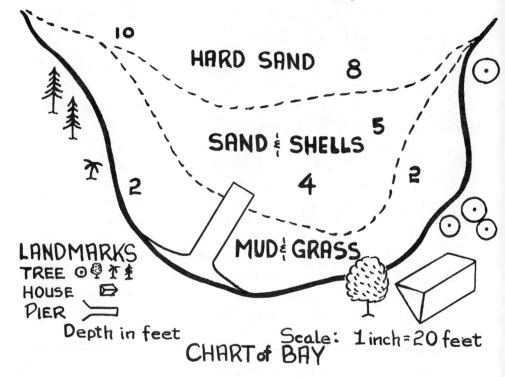

HARD SAND   8
10

SAND & SHELLS   5
4

MUD & GRASS
2

LANDMARKS
TREE ⊙ ✿ ⚘ ⚘
HOUSE ▷
PIER ⊐

Depth in feet

Scale: 1 inch = 20 feet

CHART of BAY

Picture 86 Sample chart of a small, shallow area

see which ones tend to stay in one section and which ones move about. You list the identities and estimated numbers of plants and animals. A few live specimens must be collected with a net or slurp gun to be studied in the laboratory aquariums. Because it is important to know what some fish eat, you spear a few so that their stomach contents can be analyzed. You also tag mollusca (snails, conchs, clams, oysters, etc.) and keep a record of their movements and rate of growth. The information obtained through this and other research projects will be invaluable to the future undersea farmer.

For instance, it has already been found that where there is little or no available shelter there are few fish. In such cases, man-made shelters are provided: artificial reefs made of old automobiles, streetcars, concrete, or rocks. Diving scientists check the shelters periodically and record the numbers of tenant fish and the different species. They note which types of shelter become covered with plantlife offering additional shelter and source of food and which do not. This kind of information will help the undersea farmer to house and feed his fish.

Perhaps during your years of scientific exploration you will be fortunate enough to have experiences similar to those of the well-known marine biologist, Conrad Limbaugh. He witnessed a particularly amazing example of co-operation among fish, and recorded on film and in written reports what is now known as cleaning symbiosis. He discovered that fish have a "cleaning service." When a fish is dirty or has bacteria, bits of food, or a wound on its body or in its mouth, it goes to a cleaning station. Cleaners often "advertise" to attract customers by using a darting, dancelike movement or waving long antennae. A sick or injured fish may visit a cleaner several times during one day. When business is brisk, fish will even wait in line for their turn. The cleaner removes the unwanted "dirt" by eating it, and so the payment is food. The customer fish receives the necessary service, having foreign matter or damaged tissue removed which otherwise would cause sickness, perhaps fatal. Cleaning stations may also exit in fresh water. Look for them.

Would you rather be an underwater archaeologist? Archaeology is the scientific study of the life and culture of ancient peoples. An underwater archaeologist retrieves and studies the culture of ancient peoples which has been lost under the sea.

In this field, the National Geographic Society promotes research and exploration throughout the world as does the Department of Naval History of the Smithsonian Institution.

Imagine that you are on a marine archaeological expedition to search for the remains of one of the hundreds of sailing vessels that sank in Florida waters during the sixteenth, seventeenth, and eighteenth centuries. You are a scientist aboard a large, seaworthy ship outfitted with special electronic equipment, to aid in locating a historic wreck. As you approach the possible site of a wreck, the equipment hums and buzzes and pings into action. Magnetometers search for iron buried under sand or coral. Sonar signals will show where an object is higher than the ocean floor. An underwater television camera sends pictures of the ocean floor to a receiver on board the boat. Suddenly, you are directly over a wreck!

You and your associate scientists put on compressed-air diving equipment. Then you are in the water, eager to get to work. The water is fairly shallow, only twenty-five feet deep. The air-lift tube carries sand and rubble up to the surface. A wire-mesh screen will catch any valuable artifacts. (In *Picture 87* a diver is using an underwater parachute to lift a growth-covered port cover.) The expedition is success-

Picture 87 Using an underwater parachute

ful. Many ancient items have been found: old coins, pieces of eight and gold doubloons; gold and silver jewelry, pistols and pieces of pottery. Now must start the painstaking task of removing coral crust and other growth and preserving the historical pieces. (*Picture 88*)

Picture 88 A coral-encrusted bit of "treasure"

Sometimes sport divers out for a day of pleasure accidently discover fragments of history before scientists reach the site. In fact, divers have stumbled upon prehistoric human bones, weapons made by these early men, and the huge bones of mastodons and other animals long extinct. They have discovered historically important wrecks in lakes and rivers and in the ocean not far from shore. Whenever such a find is made, the proper authorities, a museum or marine laboratory, should be notified, so that its worth and importance can be determined by scientific knowledge.

Perhaps you will want to do research on underwater sound and animal communication. This kind of research is part of the work performed by the International Oceanographic Foundation. You will learn that waves, winds, and tidal currents cause noise called sea-state noise. Marine animals can be even noisier. The sea is not a silent world at all.

Your research may take you underwater with a hydrophone (underwater microphone) that is hooked into a tape recorder above water to record the sounds made by different animals. You note which animal is making the sound being taped. By direct underwater observation, the tapes, and examination of the noisemakers' anatomies you find that these sounds are produced in many unusual ways. One noisy marine animal vibrates the walls of its swim bladders. Another grinds its teeth. Others click the joints of fin spines and snap outsize claws. The sounds produced include: croaks, bups, honks, grunts, yelps, sobs, clicks, snaps, and whistles.

Like static on your radio, some of these noises can mask out sonar signals used by submarines and warships. (Sonar stands for SOund Navigation And Ranging.) Intensive research of marine life sounds began during World War II. Marine animal noises can mask the sounds of enemy ships, perhaps even explode mines and torpedoes triggered by a certain level of sound. Research is still underway, with no end in sight.

Your research project may be the friendly, playful porpoise. This popular and intelligent mammal is believed to have a sonar system that in some ways is better than the sonar system used by the latest nuclear-powered vessels.

Your experiments require very sensitive equipment. Hydrophones and high-fidelity tape recorders are needed to record the porpoise sounds that are within the range of human hearing. (*Picture 89*) An ultrasonic recorder will transmit the sounds you cannot hear to the oscilloscope. The oscilloscope will show you the sound waves in the form of lines.

You find that the porpoise whistles a very short, very high squeaky whistle. It also makes clicking sounds which closely resemble a man-made sonar system.

You want to oberve how a porpoise locates food. You put the porpoise's favorite food fish into the water. The porpoise sends out rapid strings of clicks until the fish is in its mouth.

What purpose do these clicks serve? When you throw a ball against a wall, it cannot go through the wall but it still wants to

Picture 89 Recording porpoise sounds

move. The ball bounces off the wall and back to you. The porpoise sends—or throws out—a clicking sound. When the click hits a solid object it bounces back to the porpoise. The length of time it takes for a click to travel out and back again tells the animal how far away the object is. With this remarkable sonar system, the porpoise locates food and avoids obstacles.

But *how* does the porpoise sonar work? Continued research may answer that question and point the way to improvements and refinements in man-made sonar.

Oceanography is the branch of geography dealing with the ocean. During the International Geophysical Year, oceanographers from nations throughout the world co-operated in mapping the ocean floors. (*Picture 90*) Their findings revealed an underseascape of tremendous and unsuspected proportions. The surface of the sea hides rugged mountain ranges that are bigger than any mountains in the United States. Great gorges in the ocean floor are so big and so deep

Picture 90 Oceanographer mapping the ocean floor

that the Grand Canyon looks very small in comparison. Currents on the surface and below also were charted, as were the waves and tides that shape and reshape the shores and sometimes, when hurled forward by violent winds or undersea quakes, destroy them. All the knowledge gained, and much more, is needed to perfect marine navigation. More must be known in order to control beach erosion and to be able to predict violent seaborne storms which wash away lives and property.

But skin and compressed-air diving scientists are out of their depth in exploration below a level of approximately 130 feet. They must rely on carefully designed equipment to act as their eyes and ears underwater.

One of the underwater research vessels now in existence is the

U. S. Navy bathyscaph, the *Trieste*, which carried Jacques Piccard and Lieutenant Don Walsh to a record depth of 35,800 feet in 1960. But this type of submarine moves slowly in two directions—down and up. It cannot move for any distance along the ocean floor. (*Picture 91* shows a half-scale model of the *Trieste*, made at the David Taylor Model Basin in Washington, D.C.)

Picture 91 A model of the bathyscaph *Trieste*

Captain Jacques-Yves Cousteau's diving saucer, named *DS-2*, is smaller, faster, and more mobile. (*Picture 92*) It can move in any direction. Still, *DS-2* cannot go deeper than one thousand feet. Novel small submarines are being designed to go deeper, travel farther, and stay underwater longer than existing models.

Picture 92 Captain Cousteau's diving saucer *DS-2*

Picture 93 shows the *Link Igloo* being lowered over the side of the research ship *Sea Diver* at the Key West Naval Station. Designer Edwin A. Link and diver Robert Stenuit of Belgium are guiding the inflated house into the water. Lead weights placed in the circular

Picture 93 The *Link Igloo* being lowered

collar will hold the balloonlike structure to the bottom. In March 1964, Mr. Link was able to walk dry on the sea bottom in the air-filled igloo at a depth of thirty feet. Air pressure keeps the water out.

While these vessels are extremely useful to underwater exploration, they keep their passengers bottled up. A scientist's range of observation is confined by the craft's mechanical ability.

If men were able to move freely and stay for weeks or months at a great depth, the rich resources of the continental shelves could be tapped. Extensive, exhaustive research has already removed many of the obstacles which stand between man and the ocean floor. Men have spent days and weeks, living and working, far beneath the surface: two hundred, four hundred, six hundred feet down.

Pioneering in a new underwater world for man, French oceanauts lived for a month in a colony submerged thirty-six feet on a Red Sea shelf in June 1963. Captain Cousteau, French undersea pioneer, set up a prefabricated village (*Picture 94*) consisting of four steel struc-

Picture 94 An underwater prefabricated village

tures, several fish pens, and some anti-shark cages. Daily work of the oceanauts included catching specimens for the Oceanographic Museum at Monaco. In this picture (*94*), Professor Raymond Vaissiere (left), chief of the museum's biological division, and Claude Wesley swim near an open tool shed. A bubble of compressed air buoys each plastic bag holding live fish captured for study.

Picture 95 is of the SPID—a Submersible, Portable, Inflatable Dwelling—one of the new underwater devices designed by Mr. Link for his Man-in-Sea Project, sponsored by the National Geographic Society with the co-operation of the Smithsonian Institution and the U. S. Navy. A diver may live in the SPID for prolonged periods at depths between four- and six-hundred feet. The diver would sleep and eat in the underwater house, emerging to work on the sea bottom. The platform at the bottom of the picture holds ballast to anchor the SPID. The opening in the center is the means of entrance and egress. Air pressure inside the rubberized, inflatable section at the top keeps water out. The device carries its own helium-oxygen atmosphere in tanks shown at the top.

Picture 95 The SPID

Picture 96 shows the interior of the SPID, with Chief Diver Stenuit of Belgium, who tested the rubber-fabric, sausage-shaped underwater house. In July 1964, in a diving experiment sponsored by the National Geographic Society, Stenuit and Jon Lindbergh lived and worked comfortably on the sea floor for more than forty-eight hours at a depth of 425 feet—setting a record for depth and duration of dive.

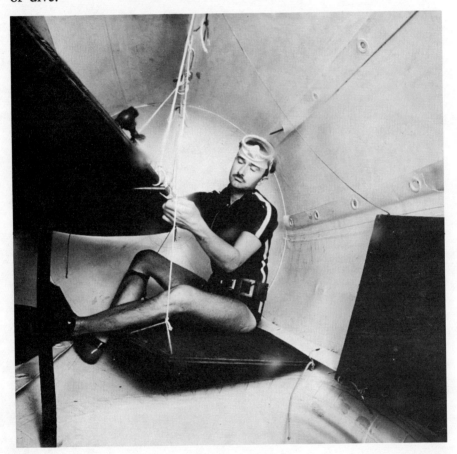

Picture 96 Diver inside the SPID

Also in July 1964, Navy Sealab divers under the supervision of Captain George F. Bond, Senior Medical Officer, and Captain Walter F. Mazzone, Senior Physiologist, lived for ten days at a depth of 192 feet in waters thirty miles southwest of Bermuda. (*Picture 97*)

Picture 97 Navy divers making final adjustments to the supply line prior to the lowering of the undersea laboratory

Small circles of light dot the dim depths. Oil drills held upright by huge rubber balloons resemble tall, skinny spiders standing neatly in a row. The drill operators seem tiny as they swim about their work under a powerful spotlight. Little underwater "trucks" glide through the water picking up and delivering heavy machinery. A farmer is tending his marine crops. Archaeologists swim off to search for ancient relics they once believed were lost forever. In his dry, comfortable laboratory, a marine biologist is happily dissecting a rare fish that was seldom seen by man.

Before many years have passed, what now sounds like a science-fiction story may have become a matter of fact. During these years some of your contemporaries, your brother, possibly your best friend, will seek careers in the study and exploration of outer space. Others will be drawn irresistibly to the underwater world—perhaps you will be one of them.

CHAPTER TEN

Safety Tips for the Skin Diver

Skin Diving:

Have a complete medical examination before you begin to skin dive. Before you dive in open water, you should be able to:

    float or bob on the surface for twenty minutes

    swim three hundred yards on the surface

    swim forty feet underwater

(do all this *without* skin diving equipment).

You will improve your personal safety and watermanship if you take a YMCA or American Red Cross lifesaving course.

Learn to dive from a qualified instructor if possible, or from a competent adult diver.

Practice all skin diving skills thoroughly in a pool or in clear, shallow water before you go into open water.

Always dive with an adult buddy—never dive alone.

Wear a safety vest on every dive.

Use a diver's flag and a reliable float.

Equalize your ears properly.

Never dive when you feel tired or sick.

Always wear a wet suit in cold water.

Always use a safety quick-release hitch on your weight belt.

Check your weights in waist-high water.

Always look up as you go up to the surface.

Keep a first-aid kit in the boat, on the shore, or in your float. The kit should contain: 4″ by 4″ compresses, gauze bandages, adhesive tape, tweezers, small scissors, small adhesive bandages, smelling salts, iodine or Merthiolate, burn ointment, an eye cup and eye wash, and ammonia. Tape four dimes to the inside of the kit along with the phone numbers of the nearest doctor, hospital, first-aid station, and police department. (You may never need any of these—but in case of an accident they are well worth having on hand.)

Learn to give artificial respiration and be sure your diving buddy does the same. The mouth-to-mouth technique is considered the most practical method.

Spearfishing:

Handle your underwater weapon with great care.

Never point a speargun at anyone on the beach—or underwater. Be absolutely sure you are aiming at a *fish* before you release the shaft.

Always remove the spearhead out of the water.

Never load a speargun on the beach.

Always load your speargun underwater.

Get speared fish out of the water right away.

Never tie speared fish around your waist.

Never spear a fish you do not intend to eat.

Always be sure the fish you spear are edible.

Wear gloves when handling lobsters and crabs.

Marine Life:

Never molest *any* marine or fresh-water animal.

Look around you—avoid swimming into or stepping on jellyfish, Portuguese man-of-war, sea urchins, and sting rays.

Stay away from fire coral.

Leave the water if you see a shark.

Never turn your back on a shark.

Stay out of the water at dawn and dusk—feeding time.

Wreck Diving:

Wear gloves.

Never go inside a wreck.

Always dive with an adult diving buddy.

Fun and Games:

Games should be supervised by an adult diver.

What About "Scuba" Diving?

You may wonder why "scuba" diving instruction is not included in this book.

First, just what is "scuba" diving? How is it different from skin diving?

The word *"scuba"* stands for *s*elf-*c*ontained *u*nderwater *b*reathing *a*pparatus. (*Picture 98*) A "scuba" diver wears a tank on his back which contains compressed air. Air is pushed into the tank under great pressure. The diver breathes this compressed air underwater. He must be very careful about how deep he goes in the water. He must be careful about how long he stays underwater at certain depths. And he must understand what happens to his body when he breathes compressed air.

Now, you probably can learn and understand all these things. But there is one important reason why you should wait until you are at least sixteen years old to dive with compressed-air equipment. *No one knows what effect such diving has on a young and growing body like yours.* Even navy doctors who work with navy frogmen are not sure. However, recent research conducted by the United States Naval Medical Research Laboratory on young goats indicates that *prolonged breathing of compressed air may cause permanent damage to young, still growing, lung tissues like yours.* Certainly, you would not want to take a chance on harming your health and physical growth.

Skin diving gives you new freedom underwater—you can skin dive for many years without running out of things to see and do.

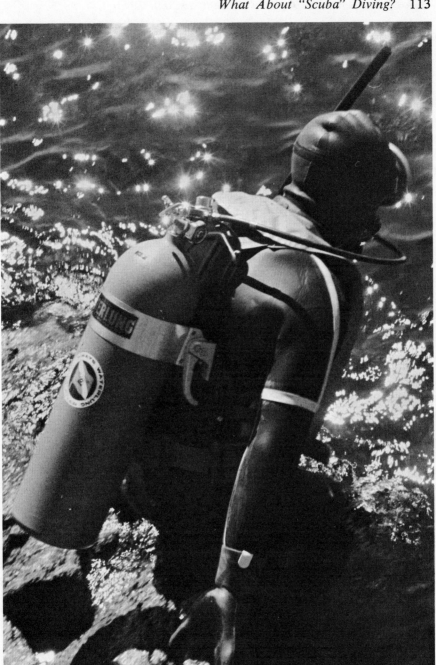

Picture 98 Diver wearing full "scuba" equipment

When you are older, your skin diving experience will help you in the more advanced sport of compressed-air diving.

Then you can enroll in a "scuba" diving course. *Formal instruction is absolutely necessary in learning this kind of diving.* There can be no hit or miss approach.

You will spend about twelve hours learning the skills in a pool, and about twice that time reading and studying the effects of compressed-air diving on your body. You will have to pass a written test before you receive a wallet-size card which states that you have successfully completed the course.

Even though a few birthdays may stand between you and compressed-air diving, you can begin to prepare for it by reading and learning all you can about it. There are many books written on the subject. A few are included in the list on the following pages.

Picture 99 "Scuba" diver and friend—one of the many rewards of underwater exploration

Suggested Further Reading

BASCOM, WILLARD. *A Hole in the Bottom of the Sea*. New York: Doubleday, 1961.

BUCHSBAUM, RALPH M., and MILNE, LORUS J. *The Lower Animals*. New York: Doubleday, 1960.

CARSON, RACHEL. *The Edge of the Sea*. Boston: Houghton, 1955.

CARSON, RACHEL. *The Sea Around Us*. New York: Oxford, 1961.

CLARK, EUGENIE. *Lady With a Spear*. New York: Harper, 1953.

COUSTEAU, JACQUES-YVES, and DUMAS, FRÉDÉRIC. *The Silent World*. New York: Harper, 1953.

COUSTEAU, JACQUES-YVES, with DUGAN, JAMES. *The Living Sea*. New York: Harper, 1963.

DUGAN, JAMES. *Man Under the Sea*. New York: Harper, 1956.

FREY, HANK and SHANEY. *130 Feet Down: Handbook for Hydronauts*. New York: Harcourt, 1961.

HERALD, EARL S. *Living Fishes of the World*. New York: Doubleday, 1961.

LEE, OWEN. *The Complete Illustrated Guide to Snorkel and Deep Diving*. New York: Doubleday, 1963.

MUNZER, MARTHA E. *Unusual Careers*. New York: Knopf, 1962.

PICCARD, JACQUES, and DIETZ, ROBERT S. *Seven Miles Down*. New York: Putnam, 1961.

RAY, CARLETON. *The Adventure Book of Underwater Life*. New York: Capitol Publishing, 1959.

RAY, CARLETON. *Wonders of the Living Sea*. New York: Home Library, 1963.

RAY, CARLETON, and CIAMPI, ELGIN. *The Underwater Guide to Marine Life*. New York: A. S. Barnes, 1956.

STEPHENS, WILLIAM M. *Our World Underwater*. New York: Lantern Press, 1962.

STRAUGHAN, ROBERT P. L. *The Salt-Water Aquarium in the Home*. New York: A. S. Barnes, 1959.

MAGAZINES FOR DIVERS:

Skin Diver Magazine, Peterson Publishing Company, 5959 Hollywood Boulevard, Los Angeles 28, California

Sea Frontiers, by membership in the International Oceanographic Foundation, 1 Rickenbacker Causeway, Virginia Key, Miami 49, Florida

Underwater Naturalist, by membership in the American Littoral Society, Sandy Hook Marine Laboratory, Post Office Box 428, Highlands, New Jersey.

You may write to the
Underwater Society of America, Bourse Building, Room 492, Philadelphia 6, Pennsylvania
for information about diving clubs and activities.

About the Author

Shaney Frey was born and brought up in Baltimore, Maryland, and trained for a career in art at the Maryland Institute of Fine Arts. But one career could never be enough for this energetic lady, and so in addition to being an artist, she is also a writer, a skin diver, an underwater photographer, and the mother of two skin-divers-to-be.

Shaney and her physicist-husband, Hank (who took many of the photographs for this book), have worked as a diving and writing team for many years, and their household is a busy center of activity and shop talk for their skin diving friends.